Assessing Science in the Primary
Classroom

WRITTEN TASKS

MIKE SCHILLING,
LINDA HARGREAVES and WYNNE HARLEN
with TERRY RUSSELL

PCP

Paul Chapman
Publishing Ltd

Copyright © 1990 as follows: Ch 1 Wynne Harlen and Mike Schilling; Chs
2 and 3, Wynne Harlen; Chs 4 and 8 Linda Hargreaves; Chs 5 and 6 Mike
Schilling; Ch 7, Terry Russell and Mike Schilling; Appendices I and II,
Wynne Harlen, Linda Hargreaves, Terry Russell and Maurice Galton.

First published 1990

Paul Chapman Publishing Ltd
144 Liverpool Road
London
N1 1LA

British Library Cataloguing in Publication Data
Schilling, Mike
    Written tasks.—(Assessing science in the primary classroom
    1. Great Britain. Primary schools. Curriculum subjects. Science. Teaching
    I. Title   II. Hargreaves, Linda   III. Harlen, Wynne   IV. Series
    372.35

    ISBN 1-85396-077-2

Typeset by DP Photosetting, Aylesbury, Bucks
Printed and bound by St. Edmundsbury Press, Bury St. Edmunds, England

A B C D E F G   5 4 3 2 1 0

Contents

General introduction to the STAR series

During the past decade, increasing attention has been paid to the provision of science in the primary school. The desire to improve the quality of this provision has been a feature not only of the educational debate in the United Kingom but also in other industrialized countries. It is, for example, the major focus of the Council of Europe's current educational programme. This attention stems largely from the realization that today's primary children need to be more 'scientifically literate' than previous generations were, if they are to solve the problems which will face them when they enter the world of work in the 21st century. The provision of Educational Support Grants (ESG) to local authorities and the elevation of science as a core curriculum area in the National Curriculum both illustrate the Government's determination to improve the quality of science teaching in our schools.

Earlier attempts to improve the provision of science in the primary school gave rise to large-scale projects funded by the then Schools Council. This approach was too simplistic, particularly in the assumption made about the willingness of teachers to commit themselves to changes which they themselves did not help to create. More recently school-focused curriculum research has tried to remedy this deficiency. However, the pragmatic approach generally adopted has made it difficult to transfer the practice developed within one school to others who did not participate in the original development.

The Science Teacher Action Research (STAR) Project has tried to combine the advantages of 'project based' and 'school-focused curriculum development' approaches. While the STAR team provided a conceptual framework for teaching science at primary level, the application of this framework, in the form of tasks which were appropriate for children of different abilities and ages, was left to the teachers who participated in the project. It was hoped that the teaching of primary science, in this way, while informed by theory would also be practical. A key element in this strategy was to provide participating teachers with appropriate means of assessing pupil performance in different aspects of the scientific processes. While the close association between what is taught and what is assessed has long been recognized, it is only recently that the positive aspects of this relationship have been appreciated. Assessment procedures which reflect the objectives of the curriculum, not only tend to ensure closer correspondence between the intentions of those who develop the curriculum and the observed practice of those who implement it but also provide a common language, based on shared understandings of the learning processes involved. Such 'shared understandings' were essential in the STAR project if the participating teachers were to play a full part in its development.

As is now generally recognized, no one method of assessment enjoys sufficient advantages over others to ensure its exclusive use. Reliable judgements of pupil performance need to take into account the capacity of children to achieve in a variety of contexts. In the STAR project, attention was given to the performance of pupils on written tasks, during practical activities and in the context of general classroom work where teachers carried out systematic observation as part of their general monitoring procedure. Each of these approaches yields information which can be entered into a profile of pupil achievement, combining the advantages and minimizing the disadvantages of each respective method.

The STAR project team was based at the School of Education in Liverpool and Leicester. The work began in 1986 and was completed in September 1989. This first book is devoted to the assessment of written tasks. For this work the Liverpool team were able to bring expertise developed while two of its members, Professor Wynne Harlen and Terry Russell, were part of the Assessment and Performance Unit (APU). At Leicester, Linda Hargreaves, in a previous project, had developed a process of assessing pupils within the context of a 'mini topic', leaving teachers free to organize the activities in ways which matched their preferred teaching strategy. The development of written assessments based on criteria reflecting the various science processes within the context of a unifying theme, *The Walled Garden*, is the subject of this book. The method offers teachers a strategy whereby they can develop their own schemes of written assessment which conform to the demands of the National Curriculum schemes of study and their related attainment targets. Although the context in which the study took place was a scientific one, the method can be applied to other areas of the curriculum. We hope, therefore, that it will serve a useful purpose for all who work in primary schools.

Maurice Galton and Wynne Harlen
Series Editors

Preface

The assessment materials described in this book were developed and used in the Primary Science Teaching Action Research (STAR) project. The project was funded by the Leverhulme Trust and based jointly at the School of Education, Leicester University and the Centre for Research in Primary Science and Technology in the Department of Education, Liverpool University, from January 1986 to September 1989.

The STAR project had the overall aim of improving practice in primary school science. It worked towards this end by involving teachers in decisions about improving learning opportunities for science in their classrooms. The particular focus of the project was the use of process skills by children in developing their scientific ideas about the world around. The starting point for making changes was a picture of what was going on in this respect in the classrooms at the start of the project. This picture was drawn by observing what children were doing in their science activities and by assessing what they could do or understand. In order to provide this information, three kinds of materials were devised: a schedule for systematic classroom observation, written assessment materials and a practical assessment task. These form the basis of the three books which the project has produced under the general title *Assessing Science in the Primary Classroom.* As the project progressed and changes were made in the classroom provision by the teachers, the assessment materials were again used to monitor the effects of the changes on the children.

In the experience of the project, these assessment materials became more than merely a research tool to provide information about the children's activities and performance. They took on the role of helping to communicate and exemplify the meaning of science process skills action. The written assessment material described here suggested to teachers the kinds of questions to ask which required and encouraged children to use process skills and which could be applied in regular activities. When teachers were involved in marking the children's responses they found themselves addressing questions of progression in skill development and recognizing the direction of the next steps which they could encourage their children to take. It was to share these wider benefits rather than merely for the sake of describing the assessment materials that we have written this book.

THE RESEARCH TEAM

The team worked from two centres:

> at the School of Education, Leicester University – Sue Cavendish and Linda Hargreaves;

> at the Centre for Research in Primary Science and Technology in the Department of Education, Liverpool University – Terry Russell and Mike Schilling,

with the joint directors of the project, Professors Maurice Galton and Wynne Harlen at Leicester and Liverpool, respectively.

ACKNOWLEDGEMENTS

We should like to acknowledge the involvement of Cheshire, Leicester, Sheffield and Wirral Education Authorities and the co-operation and encouragement given by the following local authority education advisers:

Brian Leek	(Cheshire)
Roy Illsley	(Leicestershire)
Roy Jefferson	(Sheffield)
Charles Harrison	(Wirral)

who also constituted a Consultative Committee to advise the project team. We are indebted to each authority for making available their advisory teacher teams, and would like to acknowledge the commitment and work of:

Keith Roberts (1986–7)	
Roger Walker (1986–7)	(Cheshire)
Gerry Phillips (1986–7)	
Annette Drake (1987–9)	
Sue Eland	(Leicestershire)
Geoff Tite	
Linda Gatens	(Sheffield)
Di Sutton	(Wirral)
Elaine Weatherhead	

In particular, we wish to recognize the contributions made by Gareth Williams (who was seconded to the project for the Autumn term of 1986, by Wirral LEA) and by the teachers in whose classes so much of the work was carried out: Chris Abbott Tricia Adams Jane Armstrong Anne Baird Suzanne Beard Bobbie Blakemore Lynn Brayley Lesley Broady Carol Brown Linda Burton Fred Chadwick Christine Cowlard Karen Creedon Steve Dakin Mike Delaney Alastair Dodd Jan Eastwood Jane Elders Louise Ellis Robert Elverstone Anne Ezard Peter Faragher Christine Fisher Lorraine Garnham Mark Genower Barbara Greenwood Tim Griffiths David Harker Eileen Harrigan Roger Harrison Jeremy Harwood Diane Hawkins Eddie Hunt Maraide Hurst Chris Hyland Joyce Jackson Judy Jackson Stuart Jameson Eirian Jones Dawn King Nigel Kingdon Dave Leavesley Frank Lewis Sue Lyonette Jan McDonald Paul Maddox Sue Manford Meg Marshall Martin Midgley Pam Moody Graham Morton Geraldine Murphy Margaret Noble Conrad North Janet Pilling Jan Ratherham Steve Reeds Jane Sheard Maureen Skelton Barbara Staniland Mari Street Dawn Strover Paul Stubbs Delphine Sullivan Gerry Till Felicity Titley Margaret Turner Anne Vickers Caroline Wardle Gwen Williams Mark Williams Roger Woolnough.

1

The primary STAR project

In this chapter we outline the aims of the project, its design and the instruments which were used to measure children's performance.

THE AIMS OF STAR

The project had the overall aim of improving practice in science education at primary school level. There were three distinct aspects to the work of the project:

- defining effective practice in science through systematic classroom enquiry;
- collaborating with teachers in identifying ways of making their existing practice more effective;
- developing strategies for spreading more effective practice in primary science through in-service education.

The idea for such a project was conceived in 1984 and it is worth recalling the evidence, at that time, of the need for such work. In 1984 the Assessment of Performance Unit (APU) questionnaire surveys of science at age eleven found that nearly two-thirds of primary schools spent only 5 per cent of lesson time on science (DES, 1989). In the same year, the Curriculum Provision in Small Schools (PRISMS) project (Galton and Patrick, 1990) found more science than had been anticipated in small primary schools. Eleven per cent of the observations of junior children involved some science but this was characterized by significantly higher levels of whole-class teaching and of teachers giving information and asking task questions than any other curriculum area. The teacher was the main 'resource' and about 40 per cent of pupil time was spent listening or watching (teacher demonstration or television, for example). Children spent as much of their science time copying and drawing as they did working practically. Other research published in the early 1980s (e.g. Davis, 1983), following the sharp criticism of the state of science in primary schools in the HMI Primary Survey (DES, 1978), indicated that the source of the problems was not to be found in lack of teaching materials and resources so much as in inadequate teaching approaches.

STAR had its roots in these earlier research projects. In particular, it combined the benefits of the APU work, with its strengths in novel and diagnostic pupil assessment, with those of PRISMS (and its predecessor, the Observational Research and Classroom Learning Evaluation (ORACLE) project – Galton, Simon and Croll, 1980) – which developed techniques for structured observation of classroom events while children were working. The innovation in STAR was to observe the activities and experiences of the same children who were assessed.

Although there is no doubt that many schools are severely restricted by lack of equipment and resources generally, the argument is that supplying these will not, of itself, improve primary science practice. The STAR project sought instead to focus on finding ways of helping teachers to change their practices in the direction of providing their children with greater opportunities for developing the scientific concepts, process skills and attitudes necessary to understand the world around them and as a foundation for later learning in science.

The determination to define 'good practice' within existing classrooms and to help teachers to find their own ways towards it was important for two reasons. First, because notions of 'good practice' put forward in terms of theoretical ideals generally fail to reflect the reality of competing demands on teachers' time and the many constraints which determine priorities in the classroom (Parker, 1983); only if these demands and constraints are acknowledged and taken into account will it be likely that changes in practice can be successfully implemented. Second, to attempt to change teaching approaches by beginning from where teachers are in their own practice is in harmony with the notion of improving learning through beginning from where children are in their ideas, skills and attitudes. The project's collaborative approach was designed to encourage teachers in forming an objective view of existing practice and in changing their preconceptions and skills of teaching, by looking directly at current practice.

The project had to be selective; it could not take on all the problems which have been identified as contributing to the unsatisfactory state of primary science. The HMI report (DES, 1978), for example, mentioned widespread lack of effective school programmes, superficial teaching of science processes, insufficient attention to basic science concepts, lack of teachers' background knowledge and poor match of the demand for activities to the children's capabilities. Several of these are interconnected and, together, they seem to indicate absence both of a clear view of science education at the primary level and of ideas of how to bring it about. The project chose to focus on developing teachers' understanding and practice in relation to science process skills and to do this through engaging teachers in action research. The rationale for the process skill focus is presented in Chapter 3; the justification for the 'action research' approach is made in the next section of this chapter, followed by an outline of the research programme and a discussion of the two main research procedures: pupil assessment and systematic classroom observation.

THE ACTION RESEARCH DESIGN

The STAR project objective of 'collaborating with teachers in identifying ways of making their existing practice more effective' (p. 1) encapsulated the notion of action research. This built on the idea of 'the teacher as researcher' (Stenhouse, 1975). It was important for teachers not only to be able to review their current practice objectively, but also for them to have responsibility for making decisions about how to change their teaching. Strategies for improving effectiveness developed from opportunities for shared reflection between teachers on their own classroom activity. This participative learning by teachers was designed to foster a commitment to change and an 'ownership' by teachers of the ideas for change.

However, the project organizers felt that the starting point had to be information about what was happening in classrooms. This information was collected from over forty classrooms in the initial stages and fed back to teachers as a basis for reflection.

The project's work in schools was organized in three phases, coinciding with the three school years from September 1986 (see Figure 1.1). These phases were preceded by a 'setting-up' period in which detailed negotiations were held with the four LEAs in which the project was to work: Cheshire, Leicester, Sheffield and Wirral. It was also the period in which the research instruments were devised and trialled.

Initially there were about twelve junior (composed mostly of nine- to eleven-year-olds) classes taking part in each LEA. The LEAs also made available to the project either some of the time of their primary science advisory teachers or that of seconded teachers. These teachers became part of the extended research team, helping to gather the data on the teaching and on pupil performance.

The first phase was to be the 'non-action' period as far as the teachers involved were concerned, in which baseline data were gathered about the teaching and learning in their classrooms. During this phase the teachers were not involved in any action other than making their science lessons available for observation and enabling their pupils' science process skills to be assessed. This is not a comfortable role for teachers to adopt with regard to research, but efforts were made to explain the reason for this course of action and there was the promise of active involvement at the end of Phase one. The information that had been gathered about the class activities and the children's performance was presented

Figure 1.1   *STAR project timetable*

		Project timetable
PHASE ONE	Autumn 1986	Pupil assessment using written material Observations in 'Group A' classes Practical assessment
	Summer 1987	Analysis of results Conference with 'Group A' teachers
PHASE TWO	Autumn 1987	Assessment and observations (as in phase one) Modification of practice through interventions by 'Group A' teachers Discussions between observers and teachers; self-monitoring, aided by observations Meetings of 'Group A' with project team: structured reflection, sharing of experience
	Summer 1988	'Group B' selection Conference with 'Group A' teachers
PHASE ONE	Autumn 1988	'Group A' supports 'Group B' in assessment and observations (as in phases one and two) Project team supports 'Group A' in preparing and running meetings and workshops with 'Group B' teachers
	Summer 1989	Preparation of reports on effective teaching strategies

to the teachers at an extended conference in September 1987, which marked the transition from Phase one to Phase two. In the second phase the same teachers were involved as took part in the first phase and, in the event, the LEAs made the same 'extended research team' members available. Frequent meetings between research team members (including the LEA members) and teachers, either in LEA group meetings or on a one-to-one basis in classrooms, characterized this phase. The conference marked the first of these meetings and provided the opportunity for researchers and teachers to share their views about classroom practice in science. The classrooms then became the place where strategies were critically reviewed by the teachers, each deciding the focus and goals according to their views of what was possible.

One teacher decided that:

> My priority areas for intervention should be . . . raising questions, planning (especially the understanding of controls) and hypothesizing.

Another identified:

> a need for more observational work requiring detailed rather than general observations.

The information on which teachers could make these decisions came from a variety of sources: the data obtained in Phase one provided knowledge about where the pupils were in certain aspects of their science development; input from the team and exchange of ideas with other teachers resulted in suggestions for increased opportunities for process skill use and development within science activities. Science sessions were then observed as teachers attempted to implement their planned changes, and at the end of each session the observers provided feedback about what had taken place. Teachers were thus helped to evaluate for themselves the effectiveness of the changes they were implementing.

The transition from Phase two to Phase three was marked by a second conference of all teachers, at which attention turned to the issue of how the teachers' experience of changing their own practice could be used to help other teachers work towards more effective science teaching. The strategies for change experienced in Phase two were collectively evaluated by the teachers in the light of the research data collected, to identify what had been found to be effective in various circumstances.

For the third and final phase of the project the teachers each identified a colleague for whom they would adopt the role of 'peer tutor'. Through negotiation with the LEAs, a programme of release time for the first group of teachers was agreed so that they could spend time with the teachers in the second group. They could have regular meetings to plan and to discuss the problems of implementing new ideas. The second group could also have feedback from assessment of their pupils and from the classroom observation, undertaken periodically by the teachers from the first group. Effective strategies for helping this second group of teachers, who were mainly from the same schools as the first group, were then incorporated by the teachers into their plans.

Throughout all these phases of the project it can be seen that pupil assessment and classroom observation were used to supply initial information and feedback to teachers. They could then base their decisions on information which was rather more objective than their own perceptions would have been, about where they and their children were in the development of teaching and learning. Assessment and observation information also provided the means for the teachers to monitor their own progress in the direction which they had chosen and for them to modify their plans if this seemed desirable. We now turn to consideration of how these two types of information were gathered in the project.

PUPIL ASSESSMENT

The means of gathering assessment information and ways of expressing the results are many and varied. Deciding what is appropriate in a particular case is best done on the basis of the purposes of the assessment. A fuller discussion of the range of purposes is presented in Chapter 2. In the STAR project, the purpose was to give reliable information about the process skills of individual children, which would be useful both to the teachers and to the research team.

Both groups of recipients used the information in several ways. In Phase one, baseline information was collected about children's performance in process skills, to be examined in detail by the research team. In Phase two the pupil assessment information was part of the feedback to teachers who therefore had to be far more involved in the process than simply being the recipients of results. Thus the teachers took part not only in collecting the information but also in applying process skill-based criteria to their children's responses. In doing so it was expected that they would enhance their awareness of the meaning of these criteria and of the ways in which levels of process skill development show in what children do and say. A description of the process skills is presented in Chapter 3.

In Phase three the information from pupil assessment served the same purpose for the second group of teachers as it did for the first group in Phase two. In this case the first group, with the support of team members where required, provided the mediating link between the assessment and the action which might be taken in the classroom.

The STAR project used two types of assessment procedures which between them covered the process skills which were the focus of the project.

(a) written form, in which the process skills were assessed separately in different questions across a range of subject matter;
(b) a practical investigation, requiring the combination of the various process skills in a single extended activity, but involving a single subject area.

Both written and practical procedures were designed to assess all eight process skills defined by the project (see Chapter 3, pp. 26–7), although the extent to which each was represented depended on the mode of presentation. For instance there was particular difficulty in assessing 'critical reflection' in the written test, while the practical mode presented difficulties in relation to, for example, 'planning' and 'recording'.

Written assessment

The written instrument was a compendium of tasks created to focus on aspects of the exploration of an imaginary 'Walled Garden'. The seven worksheets, set within a unifying theme, represented a novel approach to the assessment of process skills and were designed for class-based use with minimal need for resources.

Practical assessment

The practical test was administered to individual children by members of the research team visiting the school. Prior to the visit of the team member, teachers were asked to introduce equipment into the classroom which related to the problem to be investigated in the practical test; this equipment (plastic bottles, washing up bowl, string, cane, etc.) was similar, but not identical, to that to be used in the test. This step was taken to ensure that children had time to reach some familiarity, through unstructured exploration, with the context of the problem and would not be faced with a set-up which was completely new to them and in which they were asked to respond at short notice.

Children were introduced to the practical problem by being asked to think about and design a 'water sprinkler'. The equipment for the formal assessment consisted of an opaque plastic bottle suspended upright by a thread from a stand over a tray. The bottle had two small holes opposite each other in the sides near to the base. Water, poured into the bottle while the holes were covered, ran out in opposite streams when the holes were uncovered, causing the bottle to rotate. Each child was given the chance to observe this movement and the subsequent reverse rotation after all the water had run out. Each child was also given the opportunity to become familiar with the range of materials provided before being asked to carry out an investigation to answer a specified question.

While the investigation was in progress the researcher made a record of whether or not specified actions relating to the eight process skills were carried out. At the end of the investigation, the child was asked a number of standard follow-up questions about what had been done and found and then the discussion was further extended so as to give an opportunity for the child to make predictions, raise questions, reflect critically, and so on. Through this procedure it was possible to compile a record of behaviours which related to the full list of process skills. This assessment instrument is further described by Russell and Harlen (1990).

CLASSROOM OBSERVATION

The development of the observation instrument drew both on previous in-service experience (Harlen, 1985a) and on the ORACLE study (Galton *et al.*, 1980).

The main purpose was to gather information systematically about children's use of process skills, and the instrument developed became known as the Science Process Observation Categories (SPOC). Six pupils, observed one at a time, were the focus of the observation and were described as the 'target' pupils.

Classroom observers (members of the research team) used the SPOC schedule to record details of the context of the activity, such as the composition of the child's group, the involvement of the teacher at that moment and the number of children engaged in science. Recorded details of the use of science process skills were based on the child's actions and on dialogue with other children and with the teacher. The observer would listen to the children's discussion and note statements which exemplified use of the skills. For example, if the child said:

I think it's something to do with the amount of salt in the water ...

or suggested an explanation for an event, this would be coded as an example of *hypothesizing*; if a child said:

this one is heavier than the red one

this would be coded as *observing*.

For each target, observations of the process skills used, made in two consecutive two-minute intervals, were noted. In addition, the child's relevant non-talk activity, such as collecting equipment, making notes or measuring was recorded, along with the nature of any teacher intervention – asking for an account of progress or commenting on the child's work, for example.

Thus, together with notes about the format of the session and the resources and equipment used, a picture could be built up of the behaviour of, and process skills used by, a sample of children from each class.

The SPOC system of observation, its use and the ways in which STAR teachers adapted it to enable them to observe their own children during science activities is described in detail by Cavendish *et al.* (1990).

It is the purpose of this book to describe the 'Walled Garden' written assessment materials, to show how they were used in different classroom settings and to report and interpret children's performance. We also outline how teachers could use this information to provide opportunities to extend children's skills, basing examples on actual classroom work and identifying the links with the National Curriculum.

2

Assessment as part of teaching

This chapter begins with a brief review of the range of purposes of assessment in order to set the particular focus of this book in the wider context of assessment issues. The role of assessment in teaching and the various methods of assessment are then discussed, with particular attention being paid to the pros and cons of written assessment as used in the STAR project.

The starting premiss is that assessment, within its meaning used in this chapter, *is* part of teaching. We are defining the broad meaning of assessment as the process of gathering and making a judgement on information about a child's performance. It covers a range of ways in which such information is gathered and compared with some expectation, some standard or some criterion.

There are a great many classroom acts in which assessment plays a part within this definition. For example:

- responding to a child's piece of work, or answer, with a smile or a frown, writing a comment on something a child has drawn or produced, making an oral comment on the effort being made in PE – all very informal, but nevertheless involving the judgement of something against some level of expectation;
- keeping a record of children's development in skills, concepts and general understanding;
- looking at progress in various aspects of learning and using this in planning further help or challenges to give to children either as individuals or as a group.

Often, assessment in these contexts is somewhat informal and can be idiosyncratic; one of the values of discussing assessment is to make the process more systematic and less arbitrary. It has to be acknowledged, however, that it is not possible to make assessment entirely 'objective'. There is always some degree of subjectivity in assessment (even 'objective tests' are objective only in the marking; there is still subjectivity in the selection of questions to ask in the first place). The best way of guarding against the biases which this can cause is to be aware of the dangers and to be rigorous in applying procedures and checks.

In each of the classroom acts just mentioned there is something (the smile, the written or spoken comment, the record) which results from the judgement of the action or piece of work and thereafter replaces it. This is characteristic of assessment; the original behaviour is replaced by the results of making a judgement of it. To preserve the original without assessment taking place would mean video- or tape-recording, collecting the drawings, writing, models, etc., produced by a child – clearly impossible in any comprehensive way and in any case it would not retain the context in which the work was done. Thus the process of assessment is a practical necessity if we want to keep some form of record of a child's performance.

Assessment is also necessary for making a review of progress. Progress implies a change from one point to another and thus some comparison between two or more examples of performance. For this to have value the comparison must be of like with like. This is extremely difficult in terms of children's actual actions or products unless some assessment is made. For example, if Jo makes a model this week, how does her teacher compare this with the model she made in the preceding term, which has been taken home or taken apart? The teacher cannot compare the two models but she can compare her assessment of the models. To do this usefully she would have to use the same basis for judgement on the two occasions.

There are several possibilities for this. For example, the teacher could base the judgement on each occasion solely on her knowledge of Jo's usual model-making, or other abilities. She might, in effect, say 'For Jo this is a great effort' or 'Jo can do much better than this if she really tries.' Or she may look at chosen characteristics of the model and apply certain criteria relating to these, such as imaginative use of material, function, proportion, or whatever is applicable to the aim of this particular model-making. Or, again, the teacher may compare the model with a notion of what children of Jo's age should be producing and say 'Jo's model is about average' or 'Jo is rather below the average in model-making.'

The examples above illustrate the three main bases of judgement used in assessment; we will return to them a little later. First it is important to recognize that the choice of basis must depend on the answer to the question: why is the assessment being made? This question of purpose is paramount in assessment, for its answer determines the nature, extent and detail of the information gathered and utilized, the method(s) used to gather it, as well as the basis on which judgement is made. Each of these aspects of assessment will now be discussed briefly.

PURPOSES OF ASSESSMENT

The main purposes are as follows:

(a) For feedback to children   Praise children

The praise or encouragement offered to children is a way of communicating informally to them as to whether they are meeting the expectations their teacher has of them; it is also done more formally through written comment on work or by giving a mark or grade. Through this feedback, learners pick up signals about what is important and where their effort should be directed; as they become more mature they are able to assess their own work and to discuss their aims explicitly.

(b) For finding the starting point for teaching

It is a truism that teaching should start from where the child is. It is even more obvious viewed from the standpoint of the learner; no one can learn something meaningfully unless this is related to some earlier understanding. Thus the starting point must be what one knows or can do already. Finding this starting point for children is one of the most important roles of assessment in education.

(c) For appraising and reporting individual progress

Records of assessments made on previous occasions can be combined with current records to build a picture of change which indicates the extent of progress being made. Progress is often a more important kind of information to report than a description of children's present performance, for example to parents who may have no basis for judging whether or not this performance is appropriate, but who can recognize improvement.

(d) For reviewing class and school performance

This purpose of assessment has acquired more prominence as a result of the Education Reform Act. It is proposed that results of national assessment reported for children at ages seven, eleven, fourteen and sixteen years should be combined to provide results for schools which would be published for ages eleven, fourteen and sixteen years. The intention is to provide information to the public as a basis for making judgements about schools and LEAs. While the desirability of this may be questioned, the fact remains that it is one purpose which pupil assessment will serve. And, although not a part of the Act, it may also be that class scores are used for the purpose of comparing one class with another. Note that the information about individual children is lost once they become part of class and school statistics.

(e) For research and for local or national monitoring

Assessment is an important tool in research since the achievement of pupils is often the basis upon which the success of an innovation is judged. However, generally the pupils involved are chosen as a sample of their age group and the results have no bearing on them as individuals. To ensure that the results are not used for other purposes the children involved usually remain anonymous. This applies also in national monitoring, such as that conducted by the Assessment of Performance Unit (APU). Since, in this book, we are interested in assessment which can be used to help individual children, no more will be said about this purpose of assessment; it is mentioned only for the sake of giving a comprehensive view of the range of purposes.

THE NATURE, EXTENT AND DETAIL OF THE INFORMATION REQUIRED

It is implicit in the brief discussion of each of the purposes of assessment that the detail required for each varies. For feedback to children, and for making decisions about activities based on the present achievement of the children, the information has to be detailed and diagnostic. It is also somewhat short-lived, since action taken on the basis of it changes the situation and further assessment is required almost on a continuous basis. For appraising and reporting progress it is not possible to handle quite so much information and a more summary form is appropriate here. At the same time the time-scale for which the information is relevant is greater than for feedback and decision-making.

For the purpose of reporting on whole-class or whole-school performance, detail is much less useful; it would not be meaningful to combine fine descriptions of what individual children can and cannot do, nor to do this frequently. Thus the appropriate information would be in terms of broad generalities which would be provided on an annual rather than a daily basis. In the National Curriculum, the concept of profile components was created by the Task Group on Assessment and Testing (TGAT) (DES, 1988) for just this purpose of summary, whole-group reporting.

It seems that for the more short-term purposes – feedback and planning day-to-day teaching – information in a greater amount of detail is required than for the longer-term purposes of regular termly review and reporting of individual progress and of annual public reports about the school. It is also the case that the assessment carried out for purposes of feedback and planning can be reviewed and summarized for the other purposes. It follows that if the more detailed information is gathered it can serve all purposes, while the reverse is not the case: if the only information collected is of a general kind, the detail required for day-to-day teaching cannot be created from it.

This point was made in the TGAT report, which was the basis for policy on national assessment. The terms 'formative' and 'summative' were used for what has been described here as the short-term and detailed (formative) and the longer-term and less-detailed overall assessment (summative). In discussing how assessment could serve several purposes, it was stated:

> Some purposes may, however, be served by combining in various ways the findings of assessments designed primarily for a different purpose. It is possible to build up a comprehensive picture of the overall achievements of a pupil by aggregating, in a structured way, the separate results of a set of assessments designed to serve formative purposes. However, if assessments were designed only for summative purposes, then formative information could not be obtained, since the summative assessments occur at the end of a phase of learning and make no attempt at throwing light on the educational history of the pupil.
>
> (DES, 1988, para 25)

THE BASIS OF JUDGEMENTS MADE IN ASSESSMENT

The basis of the judgement used in making the assessment can vary:

- Sometimes the expectation is specific to a particular child, as when a teacher gives an encouraging smile or remark to one child's response when the same response from another child might bring a frown or admonishment (child-referenced or ipsative assessment).
- Sometimes it is based on a description of what the child can do, regardless of the performance of other children (criterion-referenced assessment).
- Sometimes the expectation is based on what is normal for children of the same age (norm-referenced assessment).

Which of these is used must depend, as so much does, on the *purpose* of the assessment. For assessment relating only to one child, as when it is used to give feedback and encouragement to a child, using an expectation which is unique to that child may be appropriate. This happens frequently; teachers use it in order to prevent a sense of discouragement in children whose performance is generally below that of others. It is sometimes useful, too, when looking for progress in a child's work, but since this involves comparison of one piece of work with another it is likely that more widely applicable criteria are used.

Where the assessment is for a purpose which involves comparison of child with child or the combination of assessments from several children, then it is essential to use a basis for judgement which is the same for all children. The 'norm' has frequently been used in the past, but this only informs about the position of a child in relation to others. It is useful for competitive selection purposes and for comparisons. Assessment based on the performance of the norma, or on the average child, indicates how an individual compares with this average, but not what he or she can or cannot do. For the latter, criterion-referenced assessment is more useful. This allows each child's performance to be compared with statements indicating various levels of achievement or types of behaviour or knowledge, and the result is independent of what others can or cannot do.

THE ROLE OF ASSESSMENT IN TEACHING

In this book we are concerned with assessment for formative purposes, where it takes an important part in teaching. Teaching which aspires to build upon children's existing skills, ideas and attitudes, using these as a basis for selecting learning experiences, must include some means for knowing what the skills, ideas and attitudes of the children actually are.

This process of gathering information and using it in teaching is familiar to teachers in many areas of the curriculum, for example in assessing reading skills, to ensure the provision of appropriate reading material. It is less familiar in science, for a whole range of reasons. One reason must be the severely restricted incidence of good practice in primary science and the low priority accorded to it before the National Curriculum brought it into the 'core'. Another reason is that, until relatively recently, not much had been done towards identifying the meaning of 'progress' in primary science so that it was difficult for teachers to interpret information about children in terms of their point in the progressive development of skills and ideas.

We now have, in the National Curriculum, explicit statements of 'Levels' in progression towards the Attainment Targets. There is also the obligation to assess children in relation to these targets and to report this at the end of the Key Stages. Since the Attainment Targets are designed to arise from the Programmes of Study, the assessment is curriculum-linked and is designed to be used as part of teaching.

Apart from these legal requirements, there are several points in favour of the formative use of assessment, which can be summarized as follows:

- It provides feedback which teachers can use to 'match' the help and activities children are given to their needs, as indicated by their existing skills, ideas and attitudes.
- Children's performances are not necessarily consistent across different activities and different learning situations. By regular monitoring, it is

possible to identify those factors that help children's progress and those that hinder it.

- It facilitates a situation in which teachers can be experimental and exploratory in their teaching, rather than prejudging what may interest children or what they will be able to do. Teachers can offer challenges which stretch children and, by gathering feedback, can be in a position to modify the challenge if it is too advanced or, indeed, too simple.
- By making some systematic recording of children's performance at regular intervals, information is accumulated which enables judgements to be made about children's progress.

However, we must also recognize points which are sometimes expressed against assessment. For example:

The child may not be able to perform a particular task, not because (s)he lacks the ability, but because (s)he's not been given opportunity to develop that ability.

Some children have a supporting home background and will show greater achievement than those who do not, so it's the homes which are different, not the children.

Statements such as these imply some sort of notion that assessment is only 'fair' if children have all had equal opportunity in all matters which affect their performance. They also suggest that the result of the assessment is to label the children and to mistake *attainment* for *potential*. We should seriously consider the warnings which are sounded here:

- First, it is very important *not* to label children as a result of formative assessment.
- Second, we must distinguish between the assessment and the interpretation and use of the assessment.

The avoidance of labelling is essential for assessment to be used effectively to help children. The response to the assessment has to be in terms of 'what can be done to help the child's progress, knowing where he is now' and not, for example, 'this child is below average/has only reached Level x/is a slow learner/ can't do this . . .'.

The fact that there will be a whole variety of reasons (some outside the control of the school) for the child's present performance is *not* a reason for assessing what the child can do, nor for ignoring assessment information on the ground that 'it's not his fault'. Rather, it is a strong argument in favour of knowing where the child is and being as aware as possible of his skills, ideas and attitudes so that help can be targeted effectively. Without this information there is considerably less chance of providing the necessary help.

A further point which leads to some suspicion about the value of assessment is that, to be useful in a formative sense, it is inevitably analytical. If we recall Jo's model, for a moment, the overall statements ('good effort', 'about average') which might be made give little information to a teacher seeking ways of helping Jo's progress. However, if there is an assessment of various aspects (choice of material, skill in construction, function, surface decoration, etc.), then there is the basis for action which might stimulate progress.

The strength of this analytical assessment is sometimes the source of objection to it. One such objection is that the parts do not necessarily make up the whole. There is no doubt that this is as true in relation to a scientific investigation as it is to a model or a painting. It is particularly important in relation to scientific skills, which, because they always have to be used in relation to some content, are influenced by what the content is. It is known, for example, that there is a considerable gender difference in response to certain subject matter. Girls will tend to engage less readily than boys in activities involving mechanical devices and the reverse will be true in relation to some life processes. Thus an assessment of ability to observe detail, raise questions, etc., will be likely to be different if the context is the movement of toy racing cars or the growth of mung beans.

Therefore, although it is necessary to know the performance in separate aspects of scientific performance, it is important to interpret these in the context of the whole activity and to keep in mind the interrelationship between the parts.

METHODS AND CONTEXTS OF ASSESSMENT

All methods of assessment, however formal or informal, can be described in terms of component parts (based on Harlen, 1983, p. 16):

- how a problem or task is presented to the pupil
- how the pupil responds
- the basis for making judgements on the pupil's response
- the way in which the result is expressed (mark, comment, etc.)

The mode of presentation can be on paper, by demonstration, through speech, through film, computer or video, and so on. The mode of response can be on paper, through action, speech, creation of an artefact, etc. The three main bases for making judgements have been discussed on p. 13 (child-referenced, criterion-referenced or norm-referenced). Finally, the result may, as in informal classroom assessment, be a word or two or a gesture, or a written comment, a mark, categorization, percentage, or one of the ten Levels of Attainment in the National Curriculum.

Clearly, there is a very large range of possible methods that can be created from combining these variables, though not all are sensible and feasible. What are useful options in a particular case is determined largely by the purpose of the assessment, the age of the pupils and the ever-present requirement for validity. To be valid, the result must be determined by the skills, ideas or attitudes which it is intended should be assessed and not by other factors or circumstances.

For all children a valid assessment depends on their being given the opportunity to show their abilities and on their willingness to take this opportunity. For very young children valid tasks for assessment in science are ones which engage the children's attention and motivate them to show what they can do, through actions, talking, or other means which do not depend on their immature skills of reading and writing. These considerations lead to the conclusion that not only must the presentation avoid the written word, but also that the context of the task must be familiar and interesting. In other words, it should be as much like the children's normal classroom work as possible while providing the opportunities for children to show their skills and ideas.

While the same points apply to older children, their ability to read and write with greater fluency opens up additional opportunities – and pitfalls – for assessment. In particular, a range of tasks which are presented on paper can be given. Presentation in this mode does not necessarily mean that the children respond only by writing; their response can be to carry out practical work of some kind which may result in a written report, but need not necessarily do so.

In this book we are concerned with assessment which can be carried out through presenting tasks in the written mode, resulting in some product on paper, even though there may be practical activity in between. However, there are many reasons why science assessment should not be undertaken solely in this way: assessing what children do, by observing their practical activity and talking to them about it, is most important; and for this reason a separate book is devoted to it (Russell and Harlen, 1990).

However, with appropriate care and ingenuity, there is much useful information about children's science skills and ideas that can be gathered on paper. And, of course, it must be admitted that written assessment has certain advantages, among which are the following:

- It is possible to give children the same tasks in the same conditions, if comparability is required.
- A permanent record of the performance is available, which can be discussed, re-marked and categorized in different ways.
- The marking and categorization can be done after the event, so it does not use the teacher's time in class (cf. Observing children's performance which can only be done in the class).
- The whole process is less time-consuming than practical assessment.

At the same time, there are distinct *disadvantages* which must be acknowledged, among which are:

- The result is likely to be influenced by the pupils' ability to read and write (unless individual help is given with this).
- Only a restricted range of skills can be assessed in this mode and justice cannot be given to the whole performance of an investigation.
- Where the task is presented entirely on paper, it may be difficult for the children to identify with it and to become motivated to show what they can do.
- Although less time-consuming for the teacher during class time than practical tasks, reading and marking responses demands considerable time after the event. The value of the assessment will depend on this time being given.

Thus in designing written tasks, the challenge is to minimize the disadvantages while taking advantage of the convenience of the written form. The potential for doing this will depend to some extent on what is to be assessed for what purposes. It is useful, therefore, to turn to the description of a specific situation so that the influence of these factors in a real case can be considered.

The written tasks described in this book were devised with the purposes of the STAR project in mind. This project was concerned with the assessment of the science process skills and attitudes; the reasons for this focus are given in Chapter 3. We conclude this present chapter with an account of the purposes and procedures for using written tests in the STAR project context.

WRITTEN ASSESSMENT IN THE CONTEXT OF THE STAR PROJECT

The STAR project was an initiative in action research in which the teachers involved were active in changing their own practice in relation to the scientific aspects of their work with children. Later, each of these teachers worked with another teacher whose practice in teaching science they attempted to improve. The three phases of the project, which followed an initial 'setting-up' phase were described in Chapter 1.

There were various assessment procedures built into the STAR project programme, one of which was a set of materials for written assessment. The development and use of these materials, known as 'The Walled Garden' materials, are described in this book. These materials provide an example of a set of tasks created round a theme, involving children in some practical activity in order to respond to questions presented on paper and to which they provided answers on paper. These answers were scored by the STAR team and teachers, using procedures described in Chapters 5 and 6.

Without going into details of the materials, which are described in Chapter 4, it is useful to summarize the nature and operation of the Walled Garden tasks. There were seven sections, each relating to objects found within the mythical Walled Garden: water, walls, minibeasts, leaves, sun-dial, bark, wood. Tasks relating to these sub-topics were devised so that they required children to use process skills. Not all process skills were used within each sub-topic but they were all represented to some extent across the whole set of seven sub-topics. Some questions required children to undertake practical activities or to look up information from the class poster which was part of the material. There was no time limit set for answering and the children moved from one worksheet to another as they finished, rather as they would in normal class activities. The time for completion of all tasks was several hours and this was generally spread over a week or two. The test was administered by the class teacher and was as far as possible regarded as normal classroom work. Children with difficulties in reading the question were given help, the nature of which was recorded.

The written assessment had three rather different roles in the three phases of the project. In all phases, the information from the written assessment was supplemented by information about a sample of children based on observing children in action on a practical task. Written assessment was used, acknowledging its limitations, because it made possible the collection of information about a large number of pupils' performance in a number of tasks in different contexts and with the degree of uniformity in presentation and scoring required for the purposes of analysis. It would have been wholly impossible to have obtained such information from procedures requiring observation of individual children.

Phase one

This was a phase before the 'action' began; it was one in which baseline information was collected about the performance of the children in the project teachers' classes. Although the teachers administered the assessment, they did not score the children's answers. Findings were presented to the teachers at the end of the phase.

Thus the purpose of the assessment was to obtain information about children's process skills on a scale which made it possible for generalizations to emerge across classes and for information to be given for each class about the relative performance of children in the various process skills. These findings showed, for example, that children's achievement was generally higher in the fields of observing, measuring, and recording than in interpreting observations and results, hypothesizing, raising questions, planning investigations and critically reflecting.

Phase two

In this phase the written assessment had a key role in providing feedback to teachers about the details of performance of individuals, as well as providing a picture of the class as a whole. Feedback from Phase one had alerted teachers to the likely general picture in their classrooms, but as they now had different children it was necessary to find each child's starting point with regard to process skills. Thus the scoring of children's answers was a key activity in providing this information.

Many teachers were astonished by what their children wrote. Sometimes the surprise was in terms of what some could do which was not expected; more often it was to challenge their assumptions about children's skills and ideas and led to changes in priorities for teaching in style and in organization:

> I now pass from group to group, not speaking and making suggestions as I once did, but now listening.

> (the tests) have made me more aware of the process skills that form the fundamental basis of practical science.

> It was pleasing to note that most children had some idea of a fair test.

> Interpretation of the graph was very disappointing as they have all done similar work (in maths).

The process of reading and analysing what the children produced gave very clear messages about what the children's needs were. Any thoughts that there might be problems in identifying areas of particular need tended to evaporate, since the messages about what was required were clear from the children's responses.

Phase three

The feedback from the Walled Garden assessment had played an important part in the project teachers' decisions in Phase two and it was to play the same part for the group of teachers who became involved in Phase three. The same written assessment materials were used in the new teachers' classrooms and thus provided feedback about the children in these teachers' classes. But the assessment also served a further function in providing a language for communication between each pair of teachers. When the teachers worked together on scoring and interpreting the children's responses, discussion of the nature of the tasks and of the responses was an opportunity for clarifying the meaning of the process skills and for an exchange of ideas about how children's development of these skills could be fostered.

Thus the additional role of the assessment in the third phase was to exemplify the meaning of the process skills in terms of specific things which children may do. All assessment materials can serve this purpose to some extent, but it is somewhat more obviously served when the material is written so that both the intended and the actual responses can be reviewed repeatedly if required and when it relates to tasks which are designed to be close to normal classroom activities, as in the case of the Walled Garden materials.

3

Focus on process skills in learning science

Chapter 2 discussed in general terms the nature and role of assessment in teaching and in the STAR project. In this chapter we turn to the question of how we decided which aspects of children's achievements were to be assessed in the project. Chapter 4 is concerned with the details of the written assessment materials and procedures which were developed.

In the context of a project concerned with the improvement of the teaching and learning of science, the matter of what was to be assessed was closely related to the project's view of the aims of children's learning in science. There is no general consensus (*pace* the National Curriculum!) as to the nature of science and the nature of children's learning, so we begin by making the STAR view of these things explicit before explaining the reason for adopting a process focus in the project and in the assessment instruments it developed and used.

OUR VIEW OF SCIENTIFIC ACTIVITY

We regard scientific activity, whether of research scientists, pupils in school, or the person in the street, as having as its aim the better understanding of the biological and physical aspects of the world around. In scientific activity, there is an effort to explain observed phenomena. The explanation can only be in terms of whatever ideas are already available to the person concerned. Research scientists have advanced theories available to them, which have emerged from their own prior thinking, investigation and experimentation and from that of other scientists. Scientists communicate these ideas to each other in various journals and books and through conferences. These advanced ideas are not available to the school pupil or the person in the street; in their scientific activity they use other, less-sophisticated ideas, which arise from their previous thinking and investigation and have been communicated to them by others, perhaps in school science but more importantly through the media.

However, it can be argued that the way in which existing ideas are used to increase personal understanding is the same in all cases. What makes the activity scientific is not the sophistication of the ideas but the way in which they are tested against evidence from the world around. One way in which this can take place is when:

- the initial or existing idea is used to propose a possible explanation (a hypothesis) of what has been noticed (an observation); then
- to decide whether the explanation is really useful it has to be used to make a prediction so that it can be tested using further evidence; and
- an investigation is carried out to collect further evidence to test the prediction.

If the results of the investigation confirm the prediction based on the initial idea, then that idea becomes more useful and will be used again and tested in further situations. If, on the other hand, the evidence shows that it does not fit, then it has to be abandoned or modified.

There are many examples in science of ideas and theories being developed in this way. The idea that the Earth was stationary at the centre of the Universe, with the sun, moon, stars and planets moving round it (as proposed by Ptolemy in the second century A.D.) fitted the observations of the movement of the planets as far as they went at that time (without the aid of telescopes). But, when Ptolemy used this theory to make a prediction, the observations did not fit. As Stephen Hawking points out

> in order to predict these positions correctly, Ptolemy had to make an assumption that the moon followed a path that sometimes brought it twice as close to the earth as at other times. And that meant that the moon ought sometimes to appear twice as big as at other times! Ptolemy recognised this flaw, but nevertheless his model was generally, although not universally, accepted.

> (Hawking, 1988, p. 3)

Against this, consider some children whose explanation of metals rusting was that rust was a part of the metal, which was revealed as layers of non-rusty material were scraped or worn off. This theory fitted their observations that rust was to be found under flakes of paint on railings or on cars. But it led to a prediction that one should be able to scrape away the shiny part of a new nail and find the rust, or cut it in half and see signs of rust within. When this evidence of rust within the metal was not found, some recognized, like Ptolemy, that their idea was flawed. Others tried to adapt it or explain away the evidence.

In both these instances, we have examples of scientific and unscientific behaviour. It is scientific when valid evidence is used systematically to decide the value of ideas and an idea is given up if it is not supported by evidence; it is unscientific if the evidence is ignored, used selectively, or ideas are not

systematically tested against it. The essence of scientific activity is to brin
and evidence together, so that a theory becomes what Hawking describes as a
'good' theory:

> A theory is a good theory if it satisfies two requirements: it must accurately
> describe a large class of observations on the basis of a model that contains
> only a few arbitrary elements, and it must make definite predictions about
> the results of future observations.

(Hawking, 1988, p. 9)

But even a 'good' theory is only good as long as it fits new evidence:

> Any theory is always provisional, in the sense that it is only a hypothesis:
> you can never prove it. No matter how many times the results of
> experiments agree with some theory, you can never be sure that the next
> time the result will not contradict the theory. On the other hand, you can
> disprove a theory by finding even a single observation that disagrees with
> the predictions of the theory.

(Hawking, 1988, p. 10)

This view of science, as the search for theories which fit the evidence available
to us at any particular time identifies it as an activity in which the *processes* of
making observations, hypothesizing, predicting and carrying out investigations
to test predictions have essential roles. We will return to this relationship of
processes to concepts a little later, after first discussing our view of learning.

OUR VIEW ABOUT CHILDREN'S LEARNING

Ideas about children's learning are changing and developing just as are scientific
ideas about the world around. And, just as scientific theories can never be
proved, so ideas about children's learning are never certain and are always likely
to be changed as new evidence emerges. In this spirit our views about learning
reflect what we find to be the best explanation of observations of what children
do and say as they attempt to make sense of new experiences.

Perhaps it goes without saying that we are concerned with 'learning with
understanding' and not rote memorization. The characteristics of this learning
seem to be as follows:

- Its outcomes are ideas which are used in daily life because they make sense to
  the learner (as opposed to information which can be recalled but which does
  not relate to problems which have to be solved).
- When it is taking place, links have been created between existing ideas and
  new experience (these give both the ideas and the experience new meaning).
- It starts from, and builds on, existing ideas; so new ideas emerge from
  previous ones.

- The learner takes an active part in the creation of understanding.

This last characteristic has the greatest implications for teaching and learning. The notion that useful ideas can rarely be implanted from without, but have to be developed from within *by* the learner means that we have to help the learners with the processes of learning rather than to offer them ready-made products. It also means that it is important to find out what their starting points are, what existing ideas they have.

We have already suggested that the way in which learners construct their ideas has much in common with the way in which scientists develop their theories. Faced with a new experience, either in the classroom or in daily life, children attempt to understand it by using their present ideas. Links are formed between the new experience and ideas from previous experiences by observing similarities and differences, by words, by being encountered in similar contexts:

- Nicola decided, on seeing smooth wet wooden blocks sticking together, that the wood became magnetic when wet (quoted in Harlen, 1985b, p. 20).
- Satpal judged the speed of swing of a pendulum from how soon it stopped swinging; to him the faster it went the sooner it would reach the end of its motion.
- Sharon thought that cress seeds were a type of bean, because the only things she had ever seen being grown from seeds were beans.

In all these cases, further experience would provide the evidence for the children to change their ideas and when this happens, learning takes place. Often, communication plays a large part in this learning: exchanging ideas with others, reading, listening to how words are used by others, all enable ideas to be discussed and tried out. In science, practical investigation is important, for ideas about how things behave have to be tested in terms of whether they explain and predict the behaviour of those things. These practical activities will involve the same processes of scientific investigation as are used by scientists.

PROCESS AND CONCEPTS IN LEARNING SCIENCE

The view of learning with understanding as change in ideas brought about by the learner's mental and physical activity draws attention to the two aspects of learning: the ideas themselves and the processes by which they are tested and changed. These aspects are closely interconnected.

The ideas which are accepted at any time are dependent on the quality of the processes of testing them, as well as on the evidence available. Suppose, for instance, that the children who assumed that rust is a built-in part of certain metals tested this idea out by looking for more rust only in places where they had already found it. Their ideas would be confirmed by this evidence, but should not be, because the process of testing their theory is faulty. They are not using their ideas to predict the results of new observations. They might also confirm their ideas by either ignoring or discounting evidence ('just because we didn't find rust in one nail, it doesn't mean it isn't in others'). Clearly, the results of an investigation depend centrally on *how the processes of investigation are carried out* and the interpretation made of the evidence collected. Thus unhelpful ideas may be retained, and helpful ones may be dismissed, if the processes of testing and challenging them are not carried out in a systematic and sound way.

From this we conclude that the development of *scientific* concepts (meaning concepts which fit the evidence available) depends on the development of scientific processes of investigation and testing of ideas against evidence. The development of the skills of scientific investigation has to be supported in children through the conscious efforts of teachers, just as the development of children's concepts is advanced through planned encounters with a range of subject matter.

This relationship between science processes and concepts is represented in the National Curriculum in the form of the two profile components:

(a) exploration of science;
(b) knowledge and understanding of science.

Progression in these aspects is spelled out in the Statements of Attainment at different levels within the Attainment Targets, underlining the developmental nature of both skills and concepts. Progression in processes is a corollary of progression in conceptual understanding for, as ideas become more sophisticated and abstract, so the ways of testing them also need to become more precise, better focused and more consciously applied. Thus the development of process skills and ideas go hand in hand.

THE PROCESS FOCUS IN STAR

The STAR project chose the processes of science as its focus, not because these are thought to be more important than concepts in science or in learning science, but because it perceived a gap in understanding of how to nurture this aspect of learning in science. It can be argued that emphasis on processes is relatively more important at the primary than at the secondary level; indeed this has now been given official recognition in the weighting of the profile components in the National Curriculum. However, relatively little research attention had been given to the nature of children's development of process skills or to evaluating teaching strategies for assisting this development.

Having made this choice, we had to identify the particular processes which were to be the focus of the research. There are many ways of defining and grouping them. The origin of the STAR list and an account of some of its precursors are discussed in Cavendish *et al.* (1990). Briefly, it has its roots in the same thinking as lay behind the Science 5/13 objectives (Ennever and Harlen, 1972), many of which were transformed into lists used by projects such as Progress in Learning Science (Harlen *et al.*, 1977). Lists of this kind are also a common feature of LEA science guidelines. The value of defining separate skills within the overall scientific process was endorsed by Science HMI whose list was published in a form useful to teachers in *Science 5–16: A Statement of Policy* (DES, 1985). In its interim report (DES, 1987), the Science Working Group of the National Curriculum also produced a list of processes which, like its predecessors, was not intended to suggest that these skills are used separately, but was a convenient way of describing what comprises scientific activity.

The list chosen for the purposes of the STAR project has much in common with all these lists, but differs slightly from them in detail, as indeed they do from each other. The STAR processes are as follows:

observing	measuring
interpreting	recording
hypothesizing	raising questions
planning	critically reflecting

It is relevant to consider briefly the meaning of these in terms of pupil activity since it is this which must determine appropriate methods of assessment:

- *Observing:* taking in information about all things around; using all the senses appropriately and safely; identifying similarities and differences; noticing details and sequence; ordering observations.

- *Interpreting:* putting together pieces of information or results to identify some patterns in them or to draw conclusions; making predictions, based on a perceived relationship, which can be used to suggest what will happen at some future time.

- *Hypothesizing:* suggesting reasons for events or phenomena which can be tested scientifically by appeal to existing or new evidence; applying concepts and ideas from previous experience.

- *Planning:* proposing what has to be done to find out something through practical investigation; recognizing the variables to be controlled and those to be changed; deciding what results to collect and how to do this appropriately.

- *Measuring:* making quantitative comparisons; choosing and using measuring instruments appropriately and with the accuracy required.

- *Recording:* making necessary notes of events and results during the course of an investigation; presenting information in a helpful form and being able to understand information in various forms using graphs, charts, drawings, writing or models.

- *Raising questions:* asking a variety of questions, including those which can be answered through investigations; recognizing those questions which are investigable.

- *Critically reflecting:* reviewing procedures and results to identify ways in which improvements could be made or ideas better applied; consciously considering alternatives to what has been done and evaluating them.

THE ASSESSMENT CHALLENGE

The decision to focus on these process skills presented a challenge in relation to assessment. Many of the skills are defined in terms of *action*, so the indication is that much of the assessment must be of a practical nature. However, given the resource and logistical difficulties of practical assessment, it was important to explore the extent to which the written form could be employed. The discussion in Chapter 2 of advantages and disadvantages of written assessment (pp. 17–18) has covered many of the points to be borne in mind.

There is, however, a further issue which is particularly relevant to the assessment of process skills. Any assessment which attempts to go further than measuring the extent to which children can recall, and attempts to explore their skills and understanding, puts pupils in situations where they have to *use* their learning. But once a context is created in which the learning is to be used, the performance is influenced by that context. The impact of context has been vividly demonstrated in mathematics assessment. Given a straightforward series of numbers to manipulate, performance was almost four times as high as when the same numbers and tasks were given in the context of finding an 'average' (DES, 1980, p. 58).

Quite often there are gender-linked reactions to certain contexts, but these are only one easily detected form of difference. Others certainly exist. For example, some children perform well when asked scientific questions placed in the context of everyday life, while others do not recognize these contexts as ones which require scientific thinking. There are many examples and a useful discussion of such differences can be found in the summary of the APU Survey carried out on children at eleven years (DES, 1989).

The implications of this context effect is that children might perform differently on different questions which are otherwise very similar in the demand they place upon skills or concepts. Thus no one question or task will be able to give a reliable measurement of what a child can do, because a different setting requiring the same skills or concepts could produce a different result. The effect is present whenever a 'real' problem is given to children, but it is probably greater for the assessment of skills than for concepts. This is because the use of skills is considerably influenced by what is known about the subject matter, as well as by the context in which it is presented.

To make assessment of process skills as reliable as possible, therefore, it is desirable to have several questions, ranging across a variety of contexts (avoiding those which are known to introduce a considerable bias in respect of gender or other pupil differences). Written tasks, being more easily organized and less time-consuming than practical tasks, allow each child to be given several questions relating to each skill. Thus the STAR project, while retaining practical assessment for purposes for which written tasks are unsuitable, set about extending and exploiting the potential of written tasks for the assessment of process skills in science. Chapter 4 describes how this was done.

4

The Walled Garden assessment material

This chapter gives a description of the development, and use by the STAR teachers, of the Walled Garden material. There are three main parts to the chapter, as follows:

(a) a brief review of the value of written assessment, even in an essentially practical area such as primary science;
(b) a description of how the Walled Garden material attempts to assess science process skills on paper and of the different types of question used to enable the children to demonstrate their process skills;
(c) examples of the ways in which the Walled Garden material has been used in the STAR classrooms.

WHY TRY TO ASSESS PROCESS SKILLS THROUGH THE WRITTEN MODE?

Some fundamental justifications for employing a written form of assessment were presented in Chapter 2. These justifications can apply to any curriculum area. In summary, written assessment provides a permanent record of a child's performance; it allows children to be given the same tasks at the same time in the same conditions; and it facilitates 'time-shifting' for teachers, so minimizing any loss of 'teaching' time.

In primary science, however, we might justifiably question the use of written materials to assess science *process* skills; the teachers taking part in the project certainly did. Primary science, they contended, is essentially practical. Underlying this challenge were the two following major concerns:

(a) that written forms of assessment, such as the typical examination, and the kind of tests with which the teachers are familiar, would tend to test the child's *knowledge* of a particular area;

(b) that, since written materials depend on a certain level of language skills, children who have difficulties with the mechanics of reading, understanding and writing, would not be able to demonstrate their science capabilities.

The first anxiety was soon allayed by scrutiny of the material. It asks the children to provide suggestions, ideas and interpretations of information given. They are asked neither to provide nor to recognize facts. Experience of having participated in science activities is likely to be an advantage, but none of the tasks depends on science knowledge. The second problem is inevitable but since the Walled Garden was presented as a 'class project', and not as a test, the children could ask for help with reading, comprehension, spelling, and so on, and the teachers could make a point of helping children with particular difficulties.

We turn now to the development of the Walled Garden material.

DEVISING THE WALLED GARDEN MATERIAL

The 'seeds'

The Walled Garden material grew from two main sources of experience within the project team. Two members of the team had extensive experience of devising material and analysing responses for the science programme of the Assessment of Performance Unit (APU) and therefore knew what sorts of questions upper junior-age children would be able to tackle. The APU materials consisted largely, however, of isolated examples spread across a wide variety of separate contexts. A potential hazard of this lack of continuity of subject matter, just as in any ordinary test, is that the child sees no background context for the work.

The work of Donaldson (1978) and Hughes (1986) implies strongly that skills are best sought within contexts which give the tasks some meaning for the child: 'tasks for tasks' sake' may underestimate the child's capabilities.

Another member of the STAR team had devised some theme-based, 'mini-project' assessment materials on study skills for another research project (Galton and Patrick, 1990). These materials had been well received in the schools, and the development of a theme-based science assessment 'project' seemed to be the solution to the STAR requirements. The idea of the 'Walled Garden' emerged as a theme which could embrace several different science topics within one overall framework. A story of a class trip to the 'Walled Garden' was the basis of an introductory story for the teachers to relate when presenting the work to their children.

The contents of the Walled Garden

The Walled Garden contained seven different sections, each represented by a four-page or eight-page worksheet together with a large two-sided poster

Table 4.1 *Summary of contents of the Walled Garden assessment materials*

WATER	PLANNING a fair test to find the most waterproof of three fabrics
	CRITICAL REFLECTION on two possible methods
WALLS	INTERPRETING DATA by looking for a pattern in the number of crumbling bricks in each successive layer of the wall
	HYPOTHESIZING as to why there were more bricks crumbling at bottom of wall than near top
	RECORDING by constructing a block graph to show the number of bricks crumbling in each layer of a wall
	PLANNING a fair test to find the stronger of two building designs
	RAISING QUESTIONS for further investigation of walls
MINIBEASTS	INTERPRETING and RECORDING information in chart form
	PLANNING a fair test to find snail's food preferences
	RAISING QUESTIONS for further investigations about snails
	HYPOTHESIZING as to why there were no snails in a particular area
LEAVES	making OBSERVATIONS of similarities and differences between a holly leaf and an ivy leaf
	MEASURING the surface area of a leaf
	INTERPRETING a graph or table seeking a relationship between holly leaf lengths and number of prickles
SUN-DIAL	INTERPRETING a graph and interpolating a missing entry in an array of sun-dial shadows
	MEASURING the length of lines representing the sun-dial shadows at different times of the day
	RECORDING the measurements taken in tabular form
BARK	INTERPRETING some bark rubbings by answering questions about the texture of the bark
	PLANNING an investigation to see if a tree's bark changes from year to year
WOOD	PLANNING an investigation to test the flexibility of wood
	RAISING QUESTIONS for further investigation of wood

Wood

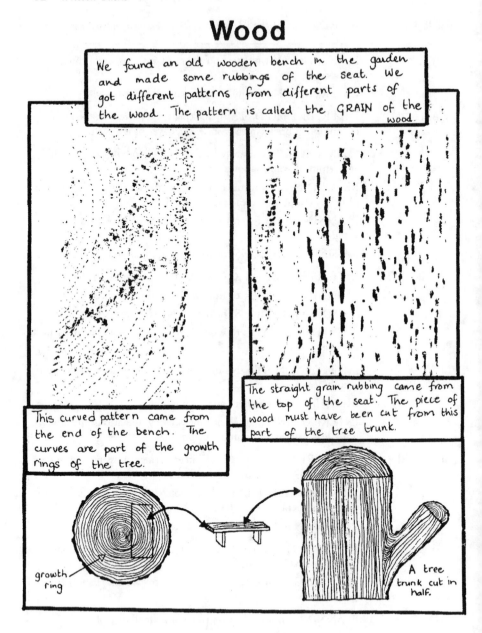

We found an old wooden bench in the garden and made some rubbings of the seat. We got different patterns from different parts of the wood. The pattern is called the GRAIN of the wood.

This curved pattern came from the end of the bench. The curves are part of the growth rings of the tree.

The straight grain rubbing came from the top of the seat. The piece of wood must have been cut from this part of the tree trunk.

growth ring

A tree trunk cut in half.

Figure 4.1   *Poster: Wood*

At school we did some more rubbings of the floorboards On some of the boards we found another pattern called a <u>KNOT</u>.

A knot is where a branch was growing.

CAN YOU SEE THE JOIN?

A joint in a desk top

A joint at the corner of a drawer in our teacher's desk.

Looking at furniture

We looked at the furniture in the classroom to find the pattern of the grain. We found different kinds of wood, with different grain. On some wood the lines were very close together. We found different colours of wood.

We looked for the joints in the furniture to see how many pieces of wood had been stuck together. We tried to imagine how the tree was cut to get each piece.

Leaves

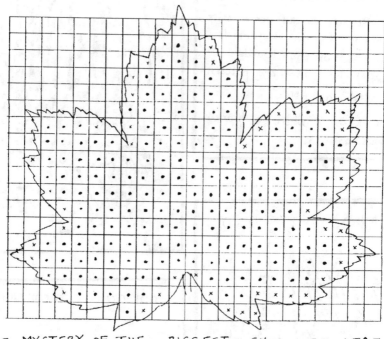

THE MYSTERY OF THE   BIGGEST   SYCAMORE LEAF.

In our group we were looking at the fallen leaves.
Everyone was trying to find the biggest. Sue found it. It
covers 241 sq. cm. but we couldn't find the tree it had
blown off. How did it get there?

We said it blew in over the garden walls. Mrs. Birch,
our teacher, said " Can such a big leaf be blown so far?
It must have blown 30 metres at least."

So she is going to bring her hairdryer and we are going
to find out whether big leaves blow further than small ones.
(Eddie says he bets it is shape not size that matters. We shall see.)

by Nicky.

Figure 4.2   *Poster: Leaves*

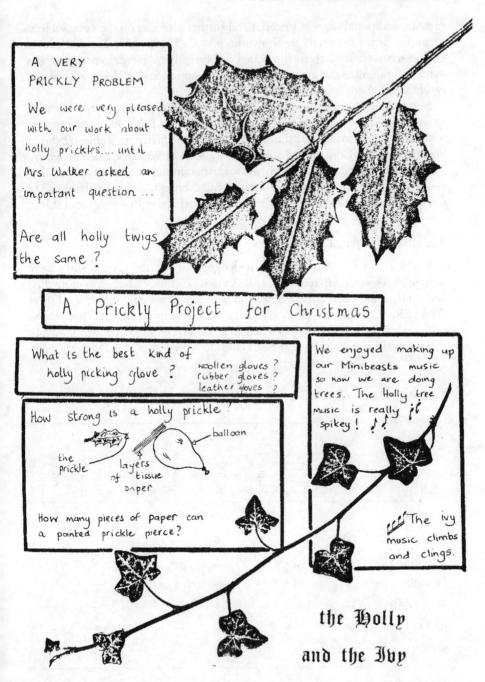

A VERY
PRICKLY PROBLEM

We were very pleased
with our work about
holly prickles.... until
Mrs Walker asked an
important question...

Are all holly twigs
the same?

A Prickly Project for Christmas

What is the best kind of
holly picking glove?

woollen gloves?
rubber gloves?
leather gloves?

How strong is a holly prickle?

balloon

the prickle

layers of tissue paper

How many pieces of paper can
a painted prickle pierce?

We enjoyed making up
our Minibeasts music
so now we are doing
trees. The Holly tree
music is really
spikey!

The ivy
music climbs
and clings.

the Holly

and the Ivy

carrying additional support material and further activities on the same subject. Examples of the materials are shown on pp. 32–5, 103–137. The worksheets and posters were attractively illustrated and brightly coloured. Every effort was made to minimize the amount of reading required and a clear, well-spaced typeface was used.

Seven sections, or sub-topics were used to create a range of contexts in which to set the items for assessing the eight process skills. In Table 4.1, the seven sub-topics and their contents are summarized, while the matrix in Table 4.2 shows how the skills were distributed across the whole set of Walled Garden materials. The numbers in the matrix simply show the maximum number of criteria that could be met for a particular skill in a particular context, but, as we shall see, the sorts of opportunities to satisfy the criteria varied across sub-topics and skills.

The range of different types of item

Tables 4.1 and 4.2 show that items designed to test the process skills were written into several different sub-topics so that skills were assessed in more than one context, although critical reflection was demanded only in one worksheet (WATER). Certain types of item construction were used to elicit some process skills, while others were approached in a variety of ways. A useful way to categorize the item types might be to consider how 'open' or 'closed' they are.

Table 4.2   *The Walled Garden skills-contexts matrix*

	Observe	Interpret	Hypothesize	Plan	Measure	Record	Raise questions	Critical reflection
WATER	—	—	—	12	—	—	—	1
WALLS	—	4	3	6	—	12	3	—
MINIBEASTS	1	3	3	6	—	3	3	—
LEAVES	6	3	—	—	3	1	—	—
SUN-DIAL	—	10	—	—	6	4	—	—
BARK	—	7	—	7	—	—	—	—
WOOD	—	—	—	3	—	—	3	—

The table shows the maximum number of criteria that could be met for each skill in each context

For example, if there were a large number of possible answers to a question, rather than one right answer we would refer to that as an open question. A question which demanded a single 'right' answer, on the other hand, would be a closed, convergent question. Such closed questions are typical of quizzes, mental arithmetic, or situations where factual recall is required. They are commonly used by teachers, too, as shown in the ORACLE study (Galton *et al.* 1980) which found that teachers asked ten times as many closed as open questions; open questions were used very rarely. The Walled Garden contained both open and closed questions and we shall consider first the skills which required open-ended items.

Raising questions and hypothesizing

Both raising questions for investigation and hypothesizing required the production of a variety of responses or ideas. A similar question format was used in both cases; the children were asked to try to think of 'as many reasons for . . .' or 'three things to investigate about . . .'. The items which required children to ask questions all followed on from planning questions in which the children had been asked to plan a specific investigation. They were then asked to think of other investigations about WALLS, WOOD and SNAILS. As we shall see in Chapter 6, many children found it very difficult to (a) formulate questions or (b) formulate *investigable* questions.

The hypothesizing tasks were slightly more focused. Something must be given to hypothesize about! In each case the children were presented with a surprising or puzzling observation and asked to suggest explanations (which could later be tested). Clearly, questions intended to encourage hypothesizing had to be open-ended because no hypothesis can be considered 'correct' or appropriate until it has been tested.

Planning investigations

Next, we look at the planning items. These were also open-ended in that many different plans could be suggested.

In five of the Walled Garden sub-topics children were invited to plan investigations, but the items contained different amounts of 'prompting' or structure. Most of the planning questions, with the exception of WOOD, were fairly open-ended. In BARK, for example, the children were presented with a very open-ended task with no prompts at all, as shown in Example 4.1(a). In contrast to this open task in BARK, the planning items in WOOD were very tightly structured, and led to answers which were clearly right or wrong (see Example 4.1(c)). In this case, in an investigation of the 'bendiness' of different types of wood, the items were in a multiple choice format so that the children had to *recognize* which features of the plan to keep the same and which to vary.

The planning item in MINIBEASTS (Example 4.1(b)) allowed the children

Example 4.1   *PLANNING items*

(a) **An open unstructured planning item**

BARK   What would you do to find out whether the bark on
                a tree's trunk changes from year to year?

(b) **A semi-structured planning item with prompts:**

MINIBEASTS   Suppose you have these foods that snails will eat:

strawberries   porridge oats   lettuce   carrot

and as many snails as you want. Think about what
you would do to find out which of these foods the
snails liked best.

a) Say what you would do to start with. (Draw a
picture if it will help.)

b) Say how you will make sure that each food has a
fair chance of being chosen.

c) What will you look for to decide which food was
liked best?

(c) **A tightly structured, closed planning item:**

WOOD   For a fair test, which of these things should they
                keep the same? (Tick any you think should be the
                same.)

                the thickness of the wood
                the type of wood
                the width of the strip
                the length of the strip
                where the load is hung

scope to produce their own experimental designs, but cued them to attend to certain points, such as whether they might want to introduce control variables, and how they would determine the result. Semi-structured planning items were used in other worksheets too, such as WATER and WALLS. In WATER, for example, a way to test the relative waterproofness of different fabrics was suggested by an accompanying illustration, and the children were then prompted to write down what they 'would look for to decide which (fabric) was best?' and how they 'would make sure it was a fair test'. Thus different degrees of structure were built into the tasks.

Making observations

Two forms of item to test observation skills were included. In LEAVES, children were asked to find three differences and three similarities between a real holly leaf and a real ivy leaf, which the teacher was asked to provide. Responses had to refer to observable features, rather than be based on prior knowledge (such as 'they are both evergreen'). The fact that each child would be looking at examples of locally available leaves, rather than 'standardized' leaves, was not considered important. Any particular idiosyncracies of individual leaves would be reported as differences between the two; the task was to compare the leaves, so *relative* observations, not *absolute* features were sought.

The second observation item, in MINIBEASTS, was not particularly successful. This item asked the children to find the main difference between the snail and other minibeasts drawn on a chart. As the project teachers rightly pointed out, it could be tackled through recall rather than observation, partly because the features of the minibeasts in the chart were not labelled. At the item-writing stage, however, it was felt that labelling would actually decrease the child's dependence on visual inspection of the drawings. A further criticism was that it was based on the observation of a picture rather than on the 'real thing'.

Critical reflection

Only one item asked the children to reflect critically on methods or procedures in an investigation; it was found to be difficult to produce questions of this type through paper and pencil assessment. In WATER they were asked to state (and to give a reason) which, if either, of two methods to investigate the waterproof qualities of three fabrics they considered to be best.

Recording and measuring

Process skills such as planning and hypothesizing require a certain degree of imagination or creativity: a variety of experimental plans or different hypotheses could be appropriate to test or explain a set of observations. For these, as we have shown, open-ended questions were generally set.

For recording and measuring, on the other hand, the burden of demand is on clarity and accuracy. The items designed to test these skills were more tightly structured and successful achievement could be more sharply defined.

In SUN-DIAL the children had to measure the lengths of the shadows recorded at different times of the day. For success in this question, children were expected to follow the recording format shown in the first entry in the table of results, and to measure the shadows to within 2 millimetres of the actual length. (This margin of error was allowed to cater for the limitations of school rulers and the difficulty of finding the exact origin of each line. Major measurement errors, such as incorrect alignment of ruler and line, or misreading of the length would be expected to fall outside this margin.)

Interpreting observations and data
The items designed to test the process skill of interpreting observations or data required the children to find a pattern or state a rule to summarize a set of observations or data and enable predictions about further observations or measurements to be made; sometimes, for some children, the pattern would be obvious; sometimes the questions prompted them to look for a pattern and they would have to 'hypothesize' or 'experiment' with different patterns in their mind's eye to be able to state whether there was a pattern in the data. We shall look at two different types of question which are shown in Example 4.2.

Example 4.2   *INTERPRETING items*

(a) An item from BARK in which the children are asked to interpret bark rubbings

---

Insects can be found in the deep splits and cracks in bark. Birds that eat insects search the bark with their long thin beaks. Look at the bark rubbings and choose **four** on which you might expect to find birds finding insects.

1 ....

2 ....

3 ....

4 ....

(b) An item from WALLS in which children are asked to look for a pattern in the data collected about the layers of bricks and so to interpolate the missing value

---

They counted the number of crumbling bricks along a certain length of wall. This is what they found.

5th layer	3 crumbling
4th layer	4 crumbling
3rd layer	
2nd layer	9 crumbling
1st layer	13 crumbling

.... Ground level

They missed out the 3rd layer from the ground. What do you think the number there was most likely to be?

Write in the number you think they found in the 3rd layer.

In BARK an unusual and interesting interpretation task was put forward. The children were asked to interpret a series of bark rubbings by matching or supplying verbal descriptions of the appearance of the bark and to predict on which trees they might find birds seeking insects in the bark.

In the WALLS example, which was a more traditional interpretation task, the children were asked to interpolate the missing value in the series of numbers of crumbling bricks.

USING THE WALLED GARDEN MATERIAL IN THE CLASSROOM

As the focus of the STAR project shifted from information collection in Phase one, to action research and in-service training in Phases two and three, so the function of the Walled Garden exercise altered slightly. In practice this meant that the major changes were in terms of the following:

(a) how many children were required to use the materials;
(b) the time allowed; and
(c) who was responsible for marking the responses.

In the first year, during the information collection phase, the teachers were asked to let every child attempt every Walled Garden topic within the space of a fortnight. There were the expected protests that the time was too short for the size of the task. This time restriction was important, however. It was intended to prevent the teachers from attempting to 'teach' or elaborate on, the materials. In this way we could obtain an overview of which skills a large sample of children found more or less difficult *without* the benefit of specific teaching. All the marking was carried out by the research team in the first phase. In the second and third phases, each teacher could decide whether to administer the Walled Garden to the whole class, or to use it with a sample of twelve children representing the range of achievement levels in the class. The teachers were then involved, in collaboration with the research team, in marking the scripts. This use of the Walled Garden had two functions: (a) it was a diagnostic assessment instrument, informing the teachers about their children; and (b) it helped the teachers to define the skills. In examining what children had written, the teachers learned how to distinguish between responses which showed a range of approximations to meeting the skill criteria. They also identified the skills in which their children, as a group or individually, needed further support.

Introducing the Walled Garden materials

Most of the teachers introduced the Walled Garden as suggested in the teacher's notes, by reading the story and showing the appropriate pages from the 'project folder' to the whole class. After this, in most classes, all the children worked on the same script for the first session. In general the teachers reported that their children had accepted the introductory story and:

> . . . felt it was credible.

> . . . believed that they were doing work that other children had prepared and were sharing their ideas.

Indeed, some classes were very enthusiastic about using the materials and, as one teacher wrote:

> . . . were delighted to be involved in science research.

Some were apprehensive about imposing the Walled Garden on the children when they could not see its immediate relevance to ongoing work. Nevertheless, and with characteristic ingenuity, they found ways to link Walled Garden up with something! One teacher made the initial introduction through a creative language session. Another said:

> I related it to 'The Secret Garden' which we had been reading – fortuitously!

In some classes, however, links with current topics were found: WATER, WOOD and WALLS fitted conveniently into a 'materials' theme in one class, while another had:

> started with the Holly and Ivy (LEAVES) as we had already looked closely at other trees – their leaves, bark, fruit and foliage – followed by BARK. This led on to WALLS as we had looked at buildings and the different ways bricks could be set. We had also looked at printing and pattern-making and this could be linked to the repetition of walls and school buildings. WOOD was really linked to the building of structures and why certain materials are used in certain instances.

Class organization for Walled Garden work

A wide variety of ways to organize the children, time and Walled Garden worksheets emerged over the course of the project. After the first session, the classroom administration of the Walled Garden was left entirely up to the teacher. The separate worksheets could be integrated into any classroom organization.

The majority of teachers started by having every child work on the same sheet for the first session, to establish the work. After this, about half the classes continued working on the same script at the same time, until all the sheets were done, while in other classes, different groups worked on different scripts. In some classes there was a progression for a whole-class beginning, through groups to individual work. One teacher wrote:

> I began by giving the whole class the SUN-DIAL sheet and we all worked on that one in one session. In the following sessions groups were given different tests to work on while I focused on other work (not Walled Garden) with a group. . . . As children continued there became vast discrepancies between the number of tests completed by each group so they were then used as individual pieces of work to finish.

In one school, during the third phase of the project, the headteacher enabled the two STAR teachers to work together. The teachers capitalized on this by having half the class work on the Walled Garden sheets while the other half carried out practical science tasks. They took turns to watch the children working on the Walled Garden and so:

> ... both teachers able to quickly get to the root of the children's learning problems – (whether it was) ... not reading questions fully – or cognitive understanding ...

Some teachers were anxious to prevent children copying from each other:

> They had very little chance of copying as I moved them into a space as far as possible, but we had already talked of there being no 'right' or 'wrong' answers so *their own* ideas would be fine.
>
> I encouraged them to do a different script from the person they sit next to, so that they worked individually.

The way in which the work was timetabled also varied. While some teachers stuck to their regular 'science' sessions, others were able to adapt the regular timetable. One teacher commented:

> I used morning sessions so that the children would feel that what they were doing was important.

The order in which the seven sheets were tackled was determined by the teacher in just under half the classes, but there was no fixed order in the rest. Sometimes there was a mixture, particularly where the content fitted in with the class topic work, or where the material was used to motivate the children:

> We began with BARK as that included a pre-sheet activity and it captured their interest. There was no particular order for the other sheets but I did leave MINIBEASTS until last as I thought it would be difficult to do and allowed the children to gain experience with the other activities first.

The children's reactions to the Walled Garden

We asked teachers to tell us about children's reactions to the materials. The following quotes illustrate some of the positive reactions:

> ... throughout all this work the children enjoyed the tests and would have chosen to work on them rather than on any other work in which they were involved!

> Generally the children enjoyed the activities, particularly BARK and LEAVES as these included a practical activity ...

> ... never had to force them to do any – always keen to do another one. Those who weren't were probably out of their depth and therefore were not made to do any more.

On the other hand, some found that the number of sheets dampened the children's initial enthusiasm somewhat and made some teachers feel that they were dragging the children through the Walled Garden. As one teacher reported:

> The children showed great enthusiasm for the initial papers. However, . . . interest and enthusiasm lessened . . . towards . . . the end.

Many of the teachers told us that they would have preferred to use the worksheets over a period of time, introducing them as a topic or skill fitted in with their teaching plans.

One common comment was that the children's enthusiasm was tinged with frustration that they could not carry out the tasks practically. In the third phase of the project, however (when the results were not being collected for research purposes), the children set about trying the investigations spontaneously before they could be stopped! To quote one teacher,

> Mostly we found that the children took to the booklets – certainly it stimulated action – some of it undertaken too rapidly for accuracy – but none of it causing the children to feel overwhelmed.

Problems encountered in the Walled Garden

There were, inevitably, numerous small specific problems, such as some children being unfamiliar with some of the vocabulary, or finding the questions ambiguous. Although the teachers were encouraged to help with problems such as these, the children did not always ask for help, so their difficulties were revealed only at the marking stage. In a few classes, there were initial misunderstandings (similar to those which are commonplace and occur with workcard-based tasks), such as children thinking that the bark-rubbing interpretations were to be carried out on their own 'practice' rubbings, rather than on the printed ones. In these cases the teachers were soon able to help.

One problem, which is almost inescapable in written tasks, is the dependence on reading and writing skills. Although the material was aimed at upper juniors and maintained a fairly low readability level, some children experienced great difficulty. This in turn prevented such children from 'getting involved' with the tasks and they soon lost interest. Clearly, this problem was more evident in some classes than in others. As one teacher reported:

> The reading/comprehension level was too high for the majority of our third and fourth year juniors to work independently; . . . (they needed help) not only in recording, but also in framing their ideas and thoughts into sentences.

These remarks emphasize the point made earlier in the chapter: written assessment alone is not adequate. In the STAR project, both observation during practical sessions and a one-to-one interview incorporating a practical investigation were used.

In the following two chapters we present examples of the children's written responses and describe how they were assessed against the criteria for success for each item.

could perhaps have been turned into investigable questions, were they to arise in a discussion about similarities and differences):

> Snails do not like the sun.

Some responses were not necessarily factually wrong but failed to describe an observable difference specific to snails:

> Most of the minibeasts have legs the snails dont

> They all eat diffren things

> ... they just grow bigger and keep the same skin

or they drew on knowledge gained from elsewhere:

> Snails leave marks behind them

> lots of other minibeasts have legs and shed their skin

In the question of LEAVES, children were provided with real holly and ivy leaves to compare and contrast. They were asked to list three similarities and three differences. In their answers, we looked in particular for attributes being assigned to each leaf, for instance, we required 'holly leaves have points on and ivy leaves are smooth' rather than 'holly leaves are dark on the top and pale underneath' with no contrasting attributes for ivy. As mentioned in Chapter 4, comparison requires relative and not absolute observations.

Similarities were more readily identified than differences:

> ... the same colour ...

> ... both have veins going down the middle and spreading out.

> They are borthe flexaple.

> ... both got a little yellow tint in.

> The holly leaf is hard and the Ivy isn't.

> The holly as got prickles which the ivy has'ent

> The holly is thiker than the ivy leaves

> The holly leaf is alot more shiny than the ivy

It proved difficult for some children to attend to what they could see; knowledge-based statements were offered:

> ... they both have someing to with Christmas

> one grows on a wall and the other does not.

> One of the leaves is off a tree.

5

Children's responses: observing, hypothesizing, raising questions, interpreting results and reflecting critically

A number of these skills are difficult to assess on paper. For example, the attempt to assess a child's ability to make hypotheses or to ask questions which would be investigable depends on the context of the question and on the extent to which the child is engaged with the situation. In a written assessment of this type, active involvement is minimal, and the propensity to think of questions for investigation, for example, might depend as much on motivation as on experience.

OBSERVING

As evidence of observation, we required descriptions based on the close scrutiny of drawings or objects, not on the recall of facts.

In MINIBEASTS, children were asked to note a difference between snails and other minibeasts, such as a ladybird, an earthworm, a slug and a woodlouse. The most readily observable difference, from the illustrations which were provided in the worksheet and on the poster, was that snails were the only ones with shells. This difference was described by children thus:

> none of the others have just one foot or shell.

> Other minibeasts don't have mobile homes.

> The snail has its home on its back.

> Snails have shels on ther back but the others have winges or nothing . . .

> None of them have protective shells exept the snail.

Other responses were more imaginative or creative but, importantly, they did not satisfy the criterion that the difference should be observable (although some

Children's performance (observing)

An observable difference between a snail and other minibeasts was noted by about one-third of children answering the question. Eighty per cent described at least one similarity between the two leaves while one difference was identified by about seventy per cent of children.

HYPOTHESIZING

In hypothesizing, children apply previous knowledge to an event and offer an explanation. The criterion for success in the two invitations to hypothesize was that children offer a *reasoned explanation*, and we invited and gave credit for up to three ideas.

In MINIBEASTS, children were asked for 'any reasons you can think of' for no snails being found in a particular garden. The responses varied in their detail. Some children were rather general in their speculation:

> There was either something in the garden they didn't like or there wasn't something they did like.
>
> . . . there is none of the food they eat

Others were more specific in presenting a reason, some of them suggesting that perhaps they had actually looked for snails before and knew something of their preferred environments:

> Because it wasn't damp or it wasn't in the shade.
>
> It may be winter
>
> Because thier were no damp places no Bricks and no walls . . .
>
> . . . the birds had eaten them.
>
> . . . snail killer . . . [might have been put down].
>
> . . . because ther were no cabaj and letuce.
>
> . . . no chalk or limestone
>
> . . . lots of animals that eat snails already lived there.

Some of the suggestions constituted valid hypotheses, but might have been based more on fantasy than on observations and experience. From these could come real investigations:

> . . . the ground was too hard for them to live under.
>
> . . . it might be a hot day
>
> . . . they might be far down in the soil

. . . it might be cold

There was no shelter; it was a small garden; the snails couldn't get over the wall or under it.

In a few instances there was evidence of a self-centred response (or were tongues in cheeks?):

Snails get very scared and worried so they hide . . .

Because the must be picthers on the wall and it skers them.

Because their not aloud.

A question in WALLS asked the children for 'two different reasons and a third if you can . . .' for bricks being more crumbly at the bottom of a wall. This seems to have been a good question for stimulating original thinking; there was, as anticipated, little evidence that children knew anything about frost-related erosion, but some imaginative and perfectly plausible suggestions were made:

All the water weres away the brick

Becuse the bottom of the wall was bilt first

Because all the creatchers make nests.

It has got all the weight on the bottom and no weight on the top.

The sun had dried the cement and the rain had softing it.

Blind people could have knocked there stick agasint it.

. . . because people could have kicked it.

People kicking footballs against it.

. . . dogs . . .

One suggestion in particular displayed lateral thinking of the highest order:

. . . they could of been using crumbling bricks at the bottom, then ran out of them, and had to use bricks that weren't crumbling.

No credit could be given for a statement which, although factually accurate, was not an answer to the question asked:

Cracks can come and mice can go through the holes and could cause serious damage in the garden.

Children's performance (hypothesizing)

It is interesting that children were more successful at making their hypotheses in the WALLS question. While three-quarters of those attempting the MINI-BEASTS worksheet made one plausible hypothesis, less than 20 per cent made a second one; however nine out of ten made one and two-thirds made two hypotheses about crumbling bricks.

RAISING INVESTIGABLE QUESTIONS

It seems more likely that a child will be inspired to generate questions through an involvement in and an understanding of a particular situation. Children were asked, in three of the sub-topics, to consider if there were any other potential investigations which they would like to pursue after engaging with one of the planning tasks. In this way it was anticipated that questions of an investigable nature might be more readily envisaged after applying thought to a planning activity, and credit was given for up to three investigable questions.

In MINIBEASTS children were asked 'What other things could you find out about snails by doing investigations with them?' (Answers gained credit for *investigable questions which avoided surgery*!) Some investigations would have been, in practice, extremely long-term, while others would be feasible in a day, without asking too much of the concentration of the investigator:

If they will go near other insects.

... what they usualy eat ...

... can they eat meat?

... what there feeding times are.

How fast they move?

Investigate if one moved faster than the other ...

... see how long it would take the to walk a serten lenth.

How long they live; where they like to live; do they live in groups

Which is the biggest and smallest.

... if they like hot or cold, whether dark or light places or wet and dry places.

... test how strong their shells were by gently knocking on them.

... how they move there eyes.

... the differents between sails and slugs.

Within this list it is seen that there are some fairly open investigations proposed, while others are quite closely defined, with variables identified.

Sometimes the question was interpreted as a 'what do you know' type, and facts were offered:

> it gos sloe and it live in a shell. it a bit slime. snails favret food is lettuce; they make patens when they moove;

> I think they like soft ground; I think they like the dark.

Some of the responses were derived directly from the information in the table in the booklet, and incidentally provided insight into another skill – that of reading tabular information.

> They have no legs. They hide eggs in soil. They dont have shed skins. Adults live on dead and living plants.

> . . . you could find out how snails shed their skin

In WALLS, the question posed was 'What other things about walls could be investigated? Write down as many as you can think of.' This was answered successfully less frequently than the MINIBEASTS question:

> . . . can walls smash with surment on;

> how they cope with difrent weather

Some proposed investigations were undesirable

> can walls kill you if you walked in to one

while other suggestions were for information retrieval or for observational activity

> how walls were used 100 years or so ago; what things walls can be made of.

> . . . you could measure the length; study different patterns and rubbings . . .

> It would be a nice idea to go and see where the bricks are made.

A question in WOOD was 'What other things can you think of that could be investigated about the pieces of wood? Write down as many as you can think of'.
  Some of the proposed questions would require an investigation although some of the variables needed defining a little more carefully:

> They could find out if they are waterproof if they are hard to break or easy to break

> How tough they are

> Weather they are good for carving . . .

> Test the wood to make wardrobes.

Perhaps what mattered more was to answer the question, without giving much thought to practicability. Some of the questions were scientific only to the extent that they required quantification of an observation:

> How heavy
>
> the thickness and the Bigest and the smallest.

Children's performance (raising questions)

Just over half of the children who attempted the MINIBEASTS worksheet offered one investigable question and one-quarter were able to propose two.

Performance was very similar in WOOD. There was, however, less variety in the ideas and very much less detail proposed; it is perhaps significant that the WOOD planning questions had been of the multiple-choice type, requiring less original thought.

In WALLS, only about one-third of the children were able to offer one question for investigation, and less than one-fifth offered a second one.

INTERPRETING RESULTS

The Walled Garden material presented children with results of observations and investigations, and thereby created opportunities to assess interpretations. Several skills are subsumed by the term 'interpretation' which were tested in the different sub-topics:

- *interpreting* information as presented (bark rubbings, graph, table);
- *interpolating* in a series (of numbers or recorded marks) and describing or justifying the decision;
- *describing* a pattern in written or numerical information;
- *extrapolating* from numerical data or inferring from written information.

In BARK, rubbings from six different trees were shown and labelled. Children were asked to *interpret* the rubbings by matching them with written descriptions. They were also asked to provide a description of one of the rubbings; giving up to *three significant features* was the criterion for success. In the description invited for the oak tree rubbing, the attributes defined, for which a mark each was awarded were:

(a) a **vertical** pattern;
(b) wide deep hollows; and
(c) narrow **high lines**.

The direction was very rarely specified. One of the few examples stated:

> . . . ridges going up the tree . . .

The distinction between the ridges or lines and the hollows or gaps was not often made:

> The bark . . . would feel bumpy and you could put your fingers in it . . .

> . . . lines far away from each other.

One or two children interpreted the question of how the bark would feel in a different way:

> The bark of the oak tree would feel sorry for the other trees that might be bing bark rubbed . . .

> . . . it would feel sore because all of the birds are pecking into the bark and geting into the holes to get the insectes.

In LEAVES children were asked to *describe* a pattern emerging from a table of numbers relating leaf length to position on twig (holly) and from a table relating number of prickles to leaf length (holly). They also had to *interpolate* – by putting a missing number in the series of numbers representing leaf length. In another question, they had to be able to *describe* the pattern in data (presented as a line graph and as a table) by stating a generalized relationship. Children were far more successful in the interpolation of a number than in offering a description of the emerging pattern (of leaf length) {, 9, 10, 9, [ ], 6, 5}:

> They are biggest in the middle. They are small at the tip and the base of the twig.

Many explanations were not wrong but were incomplete:

> . . . towards the middle they get longer in length.

> They sort of go bigger and then small

> . . . they get longer and then shoter

Most of those who attempted a description were unable to describe the important features of the pattern:

> All of the leaves were different sizes.

> . . . some of them go down as they get biger . . .

There were not many who were successful in describing the relationship between the length of a holly leaf and the number of prickles:

> The longer the leaf the more prixcles

> There's more prickles than the lenth of the leaf.

Generally, children could more easily use than describe a pattern, but there were some outstanding attempts at description:

> . . . the leaf was so long and the prickels were two times longer.

> When a leaf gets into 2 didgits it goes in ones and with 1 didgit it goes in twos for example a leaf 9cm long and a leaf 7cm long, the 9cm leaf has 16 prickles the 7cm long leaf has 14 prickles then we take a ten cm long leaf and a 11cm long leaf, the 10cm leaf has 17 and the 11cm leaf has 18 prickles.

Others were altogether more vague:

> . . . they are not the same length.

> . . . they are different sizes

A question in WALLS presented a table of numbers, showing the number of crumbling bricks per row in a wall. Children were asked to fill in the number which was missing for one row. As in one of the LEAVES questions, children were then asked to *describe how* they decided on that particular number:

> . . . I thought it would be slightly more than four not five so six.

> Because I just looked at the patterns and I missed a number out.

One question in MINIBEASTS asked for a *description* of a pattern in the table of written information, and two other questions asked for *inference* to be drawn from given written information. Successful descriptions included:

> all minibeasts with legs shed their skin, or not all minibeasts with legs lay their eggs in soil.

However, in some cases no reference to the table was made and previous knowledge was used:

> they all have files [flies]

> if they have leg they can walk very fast

There was some evidence of differences being easier to report than patterns or trends:

> The ones with legs are differnt than the overs becase they donot have legs.

Information was provided that snails are usually found in soil in which there is chalk or limestone. Children were asked to suggest why this might be. To meet the criterion for successfully interpreting this information, children needed to infer some sort of dependency on chalk or limestone. Such inferences included:

... so they can feed from the limestone.

they live on it

... it might be what they like

... they like damp places and chalk and limestone are damp.

Because they might not be able to live with out it.

becaues the snail likes eating lime stone and chalk to bild ther musels up.

I thing there is a sauce of food in the lime stone ...

Some children went further and made a link with the snail's shell

... it's good of [for] the shell

... they need chalk and limestone for their shells.

There was some interesting hypothesizing, which could not be given credit:

Maybe they need to live in chalk or limestone like a kind of air freshener because I could not live in a room with dirty air.

The snail might colecet things to make himself comfoteble.

I don't think they mind.

In SUN-DIAL, a missing shadow line had to be drawn in. The accuracy of the *interpolation* was measured, and an explanation was requested. In another question, children were asked to interpret the information presented on a line graph by labelling the axes. Children drew a missing line (to represent 4pm, when it had been cloudy) on the diagram of sun-dial shadows, and were asked how they decided where and how to draw the shadow line:

... there was space in between three and five ...

I decided by looking at the others

After noon the shadows begin to get longer ... I draw the shadow after 3.00pm and be for 5.00pm. The size of 3.00pm and 5.00pm made me do it.

I put the line halfway between 3.00pm and 5.00pm. I did the length of the line by putting my ruler from 3.00pm to 5.00pm drawing a feint line and not going over it and then I rubbed out the first line.

I decided to put it in the diddle of 3.00 and 5.00 and I draw it a bit longer than than 3.00 and a bit shorter than 5.00.

... the shadow would be very sort if there was hardly any sun ...

... because it was cloudy it would not be a very big shadow ...

Because it was in a N Eastly direction and that is near enough.

I decide to put it the beaues it not so wind a 4.00 clock some time's but is can be very bad sometimes

They were then asked to label the axes of a graph and to provide a title. For the y-axis label, both *length* and *cm* were required; for the x-axis both *time* and *hours* were required.

The length of the shadows should be written there.

Measurement in cms of the lines.

... the centimetres shoul be written ...

... the hours ...

The time ...

The time and hours of the day.

Here are the times they were taken at.

In the title, *shadow length* and *hours/time of day* were sought:

A graph to show the length of the shadows of the sundial.

A graph to show the length of the shadow at different times of the day.

... putting the sun-dial in the right place at the right time ...

Children's performance (interpreting)

The level of performance in the interpretation of BARK rubbings seemed to depend on the phrasing of the question. Two-thirds could identify the tree with horizontal ridges, but only about 10 per cent found three trees with spaces in the bark into which a finger would fit.

Although about half the children who attempted LEAVES were able to *interpolate* an appropriate number in the series which described how holly leaf length varied with position along the twig, less than 10 per cent could *describe* the pattern in the number series. Less than a quarter of the children could describe, from the data they were given, the generalization 'the longer the (holly) leaf, the greater the number of prickles it has'.

Although about 90 per cent were successful in *interpolating* a missing number in a series (WALLS), only about one-third could provide a satisfactory *explanation* for their correct choice.

In *describing* a pattern from a table of written information about different

MINIBEASTS, about two-thirds of children were successful. More than one-third were able to *infer*, from the provided written information, some dependence on limestone.

Overall, about one-quarter were successful (SUN-DIAL) in *explaining* the reason for the position of the line, and similarly for *explaining* the length. About one-third of children labelled the y-axis correctly; two-thirds mentioned 'time' on the x-axis. Only about one-fifth were successful in providing a title for the graph.

REFLECTING CRITICALLY

There was one opportunity to explore critical reflection. In the WATER script, after the illustration of two ways of testing fabrics for waterproofness and asking children to provide the plans of the two investigations, they were asked to say which method was better, or whether there was no difference and to give a *reason* for their decision. Some children preferred the first method:

> . . . because you can test more fabrics at once.

Others preferred the second method:

> I think it is more fairly because at least with this you can see if it drops through
>
> . . . in the first idea you could not tell how much acurately had soaked through as it may soak through in the same place and get a puddle underneath.

A third group of children decided that there was no difference:

> because they are the same test nerly

although the reasoning might be suspect:

> . . . because in tests there is no right and wrong.

Children's performance (critically reflecting)

Half of the children preferred one method to the other; about one in ten thought that there was no difference.

6

Children's responses: planning, recording and measuring

In this chapter we look at what was found about children's skills of planning of investigations, their organization and communication of results and their ability to measure.

PLANNING

The features of children's plans selected for attention were:

- general approach to the problem;
- control of variables;
- measurement of outcomes.

The criteria for assessing children's plans in the Walled Garden questions were based on the APU model (DES, 1986, 1989). 'Planning investigations' was one of the six categories of performance assessed, using written questions, in the APU surveys.

Planning – the general approach

In each of five scripts (WATER, WALLS, MINIBEASTS, BARK and WOOD) in which children were asked to provide plans for an investigation, we looked for *the extent to which they clearly identified what was to be investigated or compared (the independent variable)*.

In WATER, illustrations were provided to suggest two alternative ideas for an investigation to compare the waterproofness of fabrics. The questions required procedural descriptions for each of the two methods. The answers needed to indicate that at least *two different fabrics* would need to be used:

> [first idea] . . . I would collect different materials and I would drop water on them . . .

> . . . I would get three different pieces of materials the same size . . .

> [second idea] . . . I would put each fabric in turn onto the jam jar . . .

Very few children (of those who were able to tackle the question) failed to describe an investigation. There were some examples of children interpreting the question as a test of their knowledge about materials:

> . . . I would look for a mac tipe of matearll because when you in the rain you can just take it off a shake it. and the next fabric would be a rain coat . . .

Despite attempts to contextualize the questions, with a broad introduction and support material on the class posters, there were examples of children using only recall, and describing an experiment that they had previously undertaken:

> . . . I wold get some muteriul and I would put the die on it. I would look for stones and then I wold look for some petols and then I would washis and make kreses (creases) in it . . .

There was, too, an example of a certain rigour (!) in the imposition of a method for classroom investigations:

> . . . I would consontrate and do my best . . . I would try to do my best and be carm . . .

The planning question in WALLS, again accompanied by an illustration, asked for a plan for comparing the strengths of two walls. The plan needed to include reference to *two walls* with different brick patterns, as the basis for investigation:

> . . . put the same amount of bricks on each wall . . .

In this case, the question rarely seemed to lend itself to children either simply stating 'the answer' (for example, 'a strong wall is . . .'), or looking to a higher authority or source of information ('look in a book on bricks . . .'):

> . . . by asking some body ho got it right and see if it was right.

The illustrations incorporated in the WATER and WALLS questions provided children with a clue to the procedure and the equipment needed; in other words, these were 'semi-structured' questions.

The MINIBEASTS question asked children for a plan to investigate the food preference of snails and this meant that *all four foods* would have to be made available:

> . . . I would feed the snails on each of these things in turn and see which it ate the most of . . .

> . . . I would give a bit of everyone to each snail . . .

... I would weigh out all the food till they were exactly the same weight and then put them in a box with a lid and put a snail in.

Again there were examples of children who simply provided what they perceived to be 'the answer', and proposed no investigation:

... I think the porridge oats will be chosen becase they are small ...

... Snails farvet food is lettuce.

... The snail will only eat small and thin things. It cant keep it teeth grip on thick thing's. The lettuce was nice and thin so he can get a full munch.

This question invited children to draw a picture to help to describe the investigation they would perform. In this way it was often easy to interpret the intentions, to see if all foods were to be presented, to how many snails (see Figure 6.1). This inadvertently revealed some aspects of children's knowledge of snails:

... the snail will sniff what is at the end of the tubes, and what ever he chooses that he likes best.

... The snail will go to the food wat smells best.

... I would see if there are any teeth marks in each one.

Occasionally, we found examples of children being unable to detach themselves from a personal involvement in the question to be investigated, despite the richness of the contextual setting of the question. This possibly suggests a limited experience of practical investigations. Indeed, some answers hinted that, in the area of 'living things', with the exception of survey work, practical tasks have been restricted to 'ourselves':

... I would lay the fruits out on the table and taste them at about the same time every morning at about 10.30. I would do this because if you eat the food after each one you have the taste in your mouth every time you go to eat them.

... I would tack a bite of each and see what I liked best.

An open question was posed in BARK; no structure was offered to guide the children's planning. The item asked 'What would you do to find out whether the bark on a tree's trunk changes from year to year?' Answers were expected to indicate not only the *total duration* of the suggested test, but also the splitting of this *time* into *equal intervals*, for example:

... you would have to take a bark rubbing of the same tree every year ...

... I would take a photo month after month.

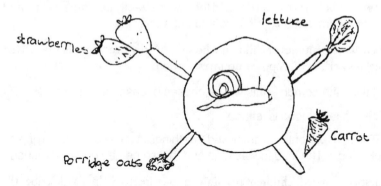

b)   Say how you will make sure that each food has a fair chance of being chosen:

The Sail will sniff ~~what~~ what
is at the end of the tubes and
what ever he chooses that he likes best

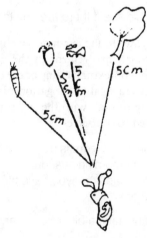

b)   Say how you will make sure that each food has a fair chance of being chosen:

put them all the same distance away

Figure 6.1   *Planning to investigate snail's food preference*

> . . . Take a rubbing during one year then the following year take a rubbing during the same month and compare rubbings.

More commonly, the time interval was stated rather than the total duration:

> . . . I would make a rubbing of one tree in January and then do rubbings of the tree every month and at the end of the year compare them and see if they had changed.

Sometimes, although an investigation was proposed, the practicability of the suggestion was not carefully considered:

> . . . each year chop it down and feel it.

There were examples where the need for an investigation was not perceived; children interpreted the question as a request for what they knew:

> . . . I think the trees bark canges every year because the tree gets older and splits and falls of. Then the tree grows more inits place.

> . . . it changes in Autum time the trunk inside has lines to tell you how old it is but you've got to have all year to count them . . .

Some children proposed that they seek help or information from an appropriate authority or source:

> . . . I would look in natrur book, dictory . . .

> . . . look throw a book . . .

> . . . I would go to the ranges office in the park and they would tell me . . .

In WOOD, the investigation was whether some kinds of wood bend more easily than others and the question was tightly structured, presented as a multiple-choice type accompanied by an illustration. The question asked 'Which of these things would be different' about the pieces (of wood) they choose to use in their test? The options listed were:

- the thickness of the wood;
- the type of wood;
- the width of the strip;
- where the load is hung.

Successful responses indicated 'type of wood' only.

Children's performance (general planning)

Only one-third of the children who attempted the WOOD worksheet were successful in this structured question. Identification of the independent variable was most successfully achieved for the first of the ideas for WATER and for MINIBEASTS, with three-quarters of respondents stating that at least two different fabrics or four different foods, respectively, would need to be compared. Of the three semi-structured questions, performance was poorest in the WALLS question; perhaps this was a less familiar context than working with water and fabrics or with snails. In response to the open question about BARK, less than one-half of children identified what was to be compared.

Planning – controlling the variables

Having considered the quality of the general approaches to investigations, we look now at some of the details within the planning. Again, different question design meant that in some cases children were prompted to consider the issue of 'fairness'.

In the sub-topics WATER, WALLS, MINIBEASTS and BARK we looked for the specification of any *'reasonable' control*; in the structured WOOD question, five suggestions were made from which the *four appropriate variables* had to be selected.

The conditions which children might have imposed in their proposed investigations for the WATER item could have included the use of the *same amount of water* on each material, *applying it in the same way* from the *same height*, and for the *same length of time*:

> . . . I would drop 3 drops on a picece of material and I would cut the fabrics to the same size . . .

> . . . by dripping two drops of water into the middle of each material.

> . . . Give each a minute or so to see if they drop through.

> . . . use the same size jar . . .

> . . . I would make sure it was a fair test I was check once again . . .

> . . . By having one percin to a peice of fabric and to bure [pour] the water on at a time.

It can be seen from the range of responses that not every identified control is necessarily relevant to the fairness of the investigation, nor is the quality of the suggestions consistent. For example, using the same size jar is only important if a non-standard measure of volume is to be made (height of water in jar) and to 'check once again' or to perform the tests 'one at a time' leaves open the question of whether anything is being measured at all. It is possible, too, that 'fairness' is interpreted in relation to equality among the investigators rather than equal treatment of the objects to be investigated, which might be the implication behind the requirement for one piece of fabric each.

In the case of WALLS, the *same number of bricks* in each wall might be specified; the *same swinging mass*, held the *same distance* from the walls, would be important. For example:

... use the same bricks on each wall or wiegh the bricks.

... Always launch the mass the same distance away from the wall.

... be the same height the same size and the same coulor and the lightness of the brick.

This last response contains another example of an unimportant or non-functional variable (colour) being identified. This child is presumably well aware of a number of similarities and differences between bricks.

In the case of MINIBEASTS, fairness might reasonably have required the *foods* to be presented *equidistant from or equally accessible to the snail(s); equal volumes* or *weights* might be presented; *numbers of snails*, their *size*, and the *time* and *order of exposure* to food could all be important, depending on the criterion chosen to decide preference:

... I would make a circle out of some string ... I would put a snail exataly in the middle and put the foods the same lenght away and see witch one he would like the best [illustrated by a labelled diagram].

... the same amount of snails and the same time.

... put the ... lettuce out one day and porridge oats the next then the strawberries the next day and the carrot the next.

... it will be fair because I won't force them to eat what I won't them to.

The last response seems to be another example of an interpretation of the word 'fair' in the everyday context of 'That's not fair ...'. Presumably, it would not be fair to the snails to force them to eat what they don't like!

In BARK, the responses to the planning question (whether the bark on a tree's trunk changes from year to year) might have included reference to the *same tree*, or the *same area of bark* on that same tree. Some children showed a familiarity with identifying those variables which it might be important to control, even if they were not important in this case:

... get some same paper all the same thicknes and take rubbings evry year.

Some just knew that this was science and that that probably meant:

... obseave it.

Often in WOOD, children were able to indicate a number of relevant variables to control from those listed. Credit was given only in those cases where all four variables were ticked (thickness, width, length of wood, position of load).

Children's performance (controlling variables)

The most successful performances were in the two WATER questions, where more than half of the children identified one relevant variable to control. Just under half identified a control in WALLS or in MINIBEASTS, while only just over one-quarter were able to do so for BARK. One-quarter of children were successful in the WOOD question.

Planning – measurement of outcomes

Identifying an appropriate measurement of the outcome of an investigation often presents a difficulty. We cannot ask snails which food tastes better, but we can observe the *numbers* of snails feeding at different food sources. We can measure the *mass*, the *volume* or the *area* (of a leaf) of different foods eaten by snails.

In each of the six opportunities for planning, we looked for evidence that children had identified something to measure (the dependent variable) and how to measure it. We used categories, as follows, to describe increasingly sophisticated performance:

1. No dependent variable is identified.
2. A qualitative outcome is described.
3. Specified outcomes are compared and contrasted.
4. Outcomes are measured and compared.

In the case of WATER, the question 'What would you look for to decide which was best . . .?' gave rise to no answers equivalent to (1). For type (2), some children suggested 'looking for the least wet':

> I would look to see if the fabrics were waterproof.
>
> . . . seeing which one had dried the quickest.

For an answer of type (3), the amount of water absorbed or passing through the fabrics was noted:

> . . . if the water would spread over the material, it was not good, or if the water went through the material it was no good at all.

An answer of type (4) could involve measuring the mass or volume of water passing through, or area of stain on the fabric:

> To see with one let the les water throgh and mesear that in the jar.

See how long the materials would last without letting water through.

Children were asked, in WALLS, 'How would you decide which wall was the stronger?' In type (3) answers (outcomes compared or contrasted) children looked, for example, for the wall which 'stayed up longer' or the one with 'more bricks remaining':

... see wich one falls down first

For type (4) they suggested counting the number of hits taken to demolish the wall, or the number of bricks displaced:

By conting how many wooden bricks are left.

For MINIBEASTS a type (1) answer gave no indication as to how to tell which food was liked best. That decision could be based on qualitative or quantitative judgements. For type (2) children said they would see which food the snails like best:

The one that it goes for

Type (3) answers suggested looking for the food with the greatest volume eaten or the one with the most snails around it:

By looking for the biggest bite in each food

Quantifying an outcome (type (4)) meant counting the number of snails choosing a food, or measuring the time spent eating:

I would weigh all the food till they were exactly the same weight and ... (after 24 hours) ... I would weigh them again and whichever one weighed the least would probably be the snails favourite.

In the BARK question, children's answers for type (2) suggested seeing if the bark 'looks different':

Feel the bark every year.

... do some rubbings each year ... and compear the rubbings

Answers of type (3) specified that changes in the pattern of rubbing, or in the distance between ridges be noted:

... take a bark rubbing every year ... and see if the pattern has changed

Type (4) contained proposals for measuring length or depth of splits in bark. There were some children who seemed unable to identify with the reality of the investigation:

... get a piece of barck and watch it.

In WOOD, the question asked 'what do you think they should measure or compare to decide the result?' Some responses were ambiguous:

> ... they should measure the wood.

Responses which were equivalent to 'how much the wood bends' were given credit:

> ... how much it has bent and how much weight it can take.

> How far down the wood bends if it snaps.

Sometimes, as with proposals for fairness, a variable was proposed which was not directly relevant to the investigation:

> The one that took the less time to snap.

Children's performance (measurement of outcomes)

While over one-half of the children were able to describe what to look for in MINIBEASTS ('type (3)') and about one-third in the other contexts, less than one in ten explicitly mentioned observing anything that would change in BARK. Less than half the respondents to BARK and WALLS identified any dependent variable (i.e. they did not suggest measuring or comparing anything). Children rarely sought to quantify anything in a manner which would enable them to apply whatever measuring skills they might possess; most common was the suggestion to *count* bricks or hits, in WALLS (one-quarter of children).

RECORDING

There is a variety of ways in which recording can be done, according to circumstances. The stage of an investigation at which a record is made will influence the nature of the record; so, too, will the purpose of the record and the ability of the children to make notes, use a tabular representation or to understand graphs and charts, for instance.

In the Walled Garden materials, tables (with written information and with numbers), a bar chart and a line graph were used to test children's skills. They were required to *construct* a bar chart, to *enter* information (words and numbers) in tables and to *read* information from a table.

In WALLS, children were asked to 'draw a block graph of the number of crumbling bricks in each layer', on squared paper. The data for the graph were presented in a table of numbers. Marks were assigned for *labelling of axes*, for *scale* and for *spacing* as well as for *accurate* (with reference to their own labelling) *plotting*.

A question in MINIBEASTS presented a table of information about eight different minibeasts and two questions were asked:

- the first question required children to *read information* from the table;
- the second question provided information which had to be *recorded* on the table in the *correct place*.

In LEAVES, information relating the number of prickles and the leaf length (for holly) was presented in a table and on a line graph. Children were then asked: 'how many prickles do you think there would be on a leaf 12 cm long?' and asked how they decided on their answer. It was possible to arrive at the right answer by reading from the graph, or by extrapolating from the table.

In the SUN-DIAL script, a drawing was presented to show how the shadow of a stick had been marked at different times during one day. Children were asked to transfer this information to a table which showed time and length. Marks were assigned for *consistency in recording*.

Children's performance (recording)

While nearly two-thirds of children correctly plotted the block graph in WALLS, the labelling of the axes was far less well done.

Ninety per cent of children were able successfully to read the information from the table (MINIBEASTS), and over three-quarters added the provided information correctly.

The correct number of prickles was determined by more than two-thirds of the children. A higher percentage of all those who answered the LEAVES question, either correctly or incorrectly, indicated that they used the table rather than the line graph.

There was almost 100 per cent success achieved in transferring at least some shadow lengths (SUN-DIAL) on to the table. Headings were provided for the columns of the table and the first entry was made in each column. Marks were then assigned according to consistency with this presentation.

MEASURING

In planning investigations, the need to identify and to measure an outcome has been described. The application of the skill of measuring is judged by the appropriateness of the unit measure selected and the accuracy with which it is used. Levels of performance in measuring range from the ability to use non-standard measures to the accurate use of complex measuring instruments.

In Walled Garden, we required children to measure the area of an actual ivy leaf and to use their rule to measure the lengths of lines, drawn on the worksheet, to represent the shadow of a stick.

In LEAVES, children were provided with squared paper on which outlines of leaves were drawn and areas (in 'sq cm') noted. They were asked to draw round their own leaf on the squared paper (centimetre squares) and to write down its area. Three marks were attainable:

- one mark for *counting all squares covered by the leaf outline which were greater than half sq cm, and no others;*
- one mark for *giving the correct area, within one sq cm;*
- one mark for *stating the units (sq cm).*

In SUN-DIAL, the lines representing the shadow lengths of a stick had to be measured, using a centimetre rule, and the lengths recorded on a table which was provided. Marks were given for lengths *correct to within 2 mm.*

Children's performance (measuring)

In the leaf area task, rather less than half the children counted the appropriate squares, or gave the right area for their leaf. Just under two-thirds reported the correct units.

Overall, about two-thirds of the children were able to measure the lines representing shadows to the required accuracy. The performance improved slightly from third-year to fourth-year children.

7

Interpreting the responses

In Chapters 5 and 6 we presented a detailed picture of children's responses to the Walled Garden questions, giving consideration not only to the skill being assessed but also to the way in which the question was presented and to the subject matter on which it was based. In this chapter we describe trends in children's performance and compare the performance of our sample of third- and fourth-year juniors with the descriptions of expected achievement in the National Curriculum Science Attainment Target One. With this information of what children can and cannot do in written assessments, and with progression as described in the National Curriculum Statements of Attainment in mind, we offer some guidelines for teachers who wish to facilitate the improvement of children's process skills in science.

GENERAL TRENDS AND PROFILES OF PERFORMANCE

Table 7.1 (a–d) shows the performance, in the eight process skills which we have described (Chapter 3), of the two age groups (9–10 and 10–11-year-olds) and of boys and girls separately. Table 7.1 shows the percentages of children meeting the criteria on more than half, less than or equal to half, or none of the opportunities presented.

Children performed better in observing, measuring and recording than in the other five process skills. Although overall percentages were lower, a very similar pattern emerged for the performance of younger children (some six-, seven- and eight-year-olds tried the Walled Garden materials in the second year of the project).

Teachers, marking the scripts of their classes, found it useful to compile profiles of class performance and of the performance of individuals. For the class as a whole, a sample, usually of twelve sets of scripts, was marked and for each process skill category, the frequency of 'successfully meeting the criterion' was

Table 7.1   *Trends and profiles of performance*

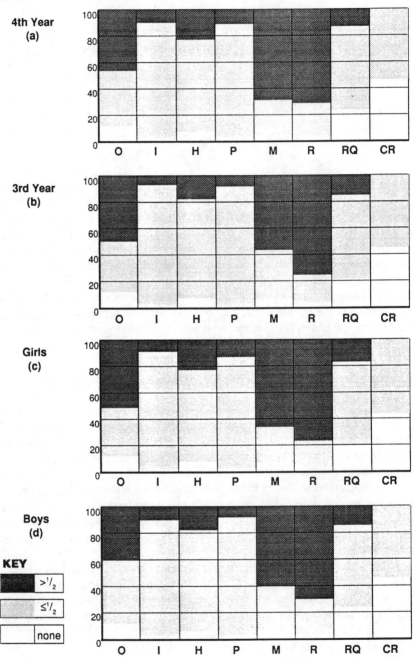

Table 7.2 *Class profile: frequency of meeting criteria for success in the process skills*

Skill:	Observing	Interpolating	Hypothesizing	Planning	Measuring	Recording	Raising questions	Critically Reflecting
Name								
Wendy	4	11	2	4	4	6	3	1
Alice	5	8	1	3	3	3	1	0
Lena	3	8	3	2	1	8	0	0
Laura	6	12	3	4	3	13	3	1
Evelyn	4	11	2	4	2	9	2	0
Debbie	4	8	1	6	5	5	0	0
Graham	3	4	1	5	3	4	0	0
Aaron	3	5	2	2	4	8	1	1
Robert	1	0	0	0	1	2	0	0
Damian	1	11	4	4	1	13	1	0
Ephraim	3	6	3	4	2	7	2	0
Neil	2	3	2	1	2	1	2	0

recorded. A chart containing the sort of information shown in Table 7.2 was completed.

The interpretation of the picture which emerged had to be mediated by two important considerations: first, each process skill was assessed by a different number of items across the set of sub-topics, so the total in each column would not be expected to be the same; second, not every child attempted every item. Nevertheless, a broad indication of capability could be discerned, which raised questions for teachers for reflection and discussion:

- Is this what I would have expected?
- Were my poor readers the least successful?
- Are there some skills in which performance has been exceptional?
- Do I normally provide opportunities for children to develop appropriate expertise in these skills?

Table 7.3   *Individual profile: performance in eight skills across seven sub-topics*

NAME	
WATER	P P P P P P P P P P P P P C C
WALLS	H H H I I I I R R R R R R R R R R R P P P P P P Q Q Q
BARK	I I I I I I I P P P P P P P P
MINIBEASTS	R I R R P P P P P P P Q Q Q H H H O I I
SUN-DIAL	R R R R M M M M M M I I I I I I I I I I
WOOD	P P P Q Q Q
LEAVES	O O O O O O M M M I I R R R I

Key: P = Planning; C = Critically Reflecting; M = Measuring; O = Observing;
I = Interpreting; H = Hypothesizing; R = Recording; Q = Raising Questions

(This profile indicates the *total* number of criteria against which responses were judged; some *pairs* of criteria anticipate alternative responses to an item; credit was given for meeting only one of the criteria in such items. See marking scheme in the Appendix for details.)

To illustrate the performance of individuals, a profile of the type shown in Table 7.3 could be compiled. This not only showed performance in the separate skills but also indicated how performance varied, in a particular skill, across the different sub-topics. By shading the items in which the child was successful, it was possible to see whether performance was consistently poor, say, in planning, or whether it was the questions about minibeasts, for example, that seemed to have produced an abnormal quality of response. This gave rise to such questions as the following:

- Does X generally know how to plan an investigation?
- How can I get Y to raise more questions?
- Why doesn't Z share explanations like these in class?
- How can I improve the level of detail in A's observations?
- Why did B and C do so poorly in the questions about Walls?
- Why couldn't anyone do the question about graphs? – we've only just done that in maths!

THE NATIONAL CURRICULUM AND TEACHER ASSESSMENT

The profiles of individual performance in the Walled Garden tasks provided measures of achievement in science process skills. The criteria for judging children's performance formed the basis for defining the eight process skills upon which the STAR project chose to focus. We now have the National Curriculum Statements of Attainment which, in Science Attainment Target One describe what children should be able to *do* in scientific exploration. In other words, the National Curriculum now provides a set of criteria which define performance in science process skills. Table 7.4 presents these statements, rearranged under the process skill headings which were used in the STAR project, to illustrate progression in the skills as described by the National Curriculum.

The trends which emerged from the Walled Garden exercise were, of course, trends in children's performance in *written* assessment. Teachers, in moderating the messages, had to consider whether, for some children, the reading or writing burden might have distorted the outcome. They had to compare and contrast the Walled Garden profiles of performance with their assessment of children's achievement in every-day class activities.

In assessment linked to the National Curriculum, teachers are making judgements about children's performance, by using the Statements of Attainment as the criteria for judging achievement. The information for this Teacher Assessment will arise out of regular class activities and will be accumulated throughout each Key Stage. In order for the information to be appropriate, teachers need to provide opportunities for achievement relating to the Statements of Attainment which are to be assessed. Teacher Assessment records will be compiled using a whole variety of contexts of children's work as the basis for judgements. The range of contexts was necessarily more limited in the set of tasks which constituted the Walled Garden material, as indeed it will be in a Standard Assessment Task. The important point to make here is that the judgements that teachers are continuously making about children's performance can, and must, make a major contribution to the overall profile of what children *can* do.

Table 7.4 *Attainment Target One*

	Level One	Level Two	Level Three	Level Four	Level Five
OBSERVING	Observe familiar materials and events at first hand. Describe and communicate observations	Identify simple differences	Describe activities by sequencing features		
INTERPRETING		Associate one factor with another	Interpret pictograms and bar charts. Use generalized statements	Draw conclusions from results	Identify patterns in data from various sources
HYPOTHESIZING			Formulate hypotheses	Formulate testable hypotheses	
PLANNING			Identify simple variables that change over time. Distinguish fair and unfair tests	Construct fair tests. Identify and control variables. Follow written instructions. Carry out investigation with regard to safety	Design investigations to answer own questions. Identify and manipulate independent and dependent variables
MEASURING		Use non-standard and standard measures	Select and use simple instruments. Quantify variables to nearest labelled division	Select and use a range of instruments	Select and use complex instruments accurately
RECORDING		List and collate observations. Record findings in charts, drawings, etc.	Record experimental findings	Record results – tables, bar charts, line graphs. Describe investigations as ordered prose, using limited technical vocabulary	Make written statements to describe data
RAISING QUESTIONS		Ask questions and suggest ideas		Raise questions in investigable form	Use concepts, knowledge and skills to suggest simple questions

INTERPRETING THE RESULTS: IMPLICATIONS FOR TEACHING

Observing

Observation involves any of the senses, but vision tends to be the mode of sensing which is used most. The Programme of Study in Science for Key Stage One states that children should experience 'at first hand the exploration of objects and events' and that they should be 'using their senses and noting similarities and differences'.

In the Walled Garden material, children were asked to identify similarities and differences (LEAVES) and to list and collate their observations (National Curriculum AT1 Level Two). While it can be reported that 80 per cent of children met the criteria for Level Two (for listing observations, if not for identifying differences), there are other more subtle criteria which might be considered by the teacher:

• Is the child able to describe fine details?
• Does the child use all senses to identify relevant features (with due caution exercised over tasting)?
• Can the child identify similarities between different objects and events; if so can s/he identify differences between similar objects and events?

Teachers expressed considerable disappointment in the level of detail offered by children in their lists of similarities and differences. Many were determined to improve performance in this skill which, it had been generally assumed, was regularly taught in science. This gives rise to an interesting point about criterion-referenced assessment; the criterion for success in the LEAVES question made no reference to the *quality* of observations, only that the attributes listed must be observable, and not factual recall. So, although the majority of children met the criterion, further work was deemed by the teachers to be necessary in order to improve the application of their skill in observing. Criteria which describe achievement need not, therefore, form a straitjacket which restricts opportunity and performance, but can offer a framework upon which to build. To develop observation in fine detail, a number of strategies and ideas were applied:

(1) Encouraging children to draw something, which is familiar to them, before they can actually see it (for example, the flame of a candle before it is lit, or a light bulb before it is taken out of its box) not only highlights missing or incorrect detail but can also lead to discussion between children about what they can see or what they have drawn. The use of a hand lens (to look at a dried flower, for example) or a mirror (to see what a face *really* looks like!) can provide the motivation to pay attention to detail. Comparative observations might then be encouraged by investigating whether all flames, bulbs or faces are the same.

(2) Blindfolding can be a means of improving the detail of what children *see*

by using their sense of touch. Many children were able to make rubbings to help them to interpret the ones which were reproduced in the BARK script. The detail that they were able to see in their rubbing could have been enhanced if they had first been blindfolded and asked to feel and describe the bark of several trees.

In looking for evidence of Attainment Target One Level Three performance (describing activities by sequencing) it might be useful to consider the following questions:

- Does the child make any notes during an investigation?
- Are notes made only at the end of an investigation?
- Is the correct sequence of events recalled if a written (or verbal) record is compiled afterwards?

The teacher might, for example, seek a verbal description of an investigation, which could be presented to the whole class as a means of sharing and comparing the practical work of different groups. A sequence of drawings or a report in the form of a set of notes could be displayed for the same purpose.

Hypothesizing

When seeking hypotheses, opportunities should be provided for children to offer explanations.

The Walled Garden questions gave an opportunity for performance equivalent to National Curriculum Statements of Attainment at Level Three (formulate hypotheses) – *testable* hypotheses were not explicitly sought, nor indeed appropriate in the case of crumbling bricks. Three-quarters of children achieved Level Three and of these a significant proportion achieved Level Four (formulate testable hypotheses) in MINIBEASTS. The criterion for success was that the hypothesis offered was *reasonable*. The questions did not seek to elicit *knowledge* about frost erosion (WALLS) or snails' preferred habitats (MINI-BEASTS), and this carries an important message for teachers' questioning of children. Questions need to be asked which do not appear to imply that the teacher is the sole owner of the answer, or indeed that there can be only one answer. In attempting to improve children's skill in hypothesizing, teachers might consider:

- Do I ever ask children: 'What do *you* think?'
- Do the children ever test their own ideas?
- Are they used to offering more than one idea or accepting more than one explanation?

The continuous nature of teacher assessment will facilitate the application of additional criteria which can be applied to children's hypotheses which arise in different contexts. For example, if an explanation is sought of a recently experienced event, the explanation should be relevant to the context and should be consistent with the available evidence. Hypotheses are not wild guesses or fantasies and care is needed in handling discussions with children in order not to be perceived as dismissed ideas without due consideration. The exploration, through discussion, of children's hypotheses can give useful insights to their understanding and, in different contexts, can provide opportunities for making judgements about children's achievement in the Attainment Targets for 'Knowledge and understanding'.

Raising Questions

Most teachers reported that their children *could* ask questions, and the teachers were therefore disappointed at the levels of performance in the Walled Garden exercise. The key issue in the context of science is whether or not the questions which children raise are *investigable*. Looking at children's responses, the significance of this criterion for success became clear.

For two of the Walled Garden items (WOOD, MINIBEASTS) just over half of the responses met the criterion for Level Four (suggestions which were investigable were made). Less than one-third of the children were able to offer more than one question. Of particular significance was the number of children who responded to a question of the type 'What would you like to find out?' with a reply which only conveyed 'This is what I know'. Not only did many children simply make *statements* but a large number asked questions which could be answered by observation and which did not lead to an investigation.

The Programme of Study (Key Stage One) states that science activities should 'promote the raising and answering of questions'. During regular class activity in science it is likely that many more questions will be encountered by, than will be generated by, children. Somehow, something seems to militate against children asking the genuine open questions typical of preschoolers – questions which are amusingly captured by Roger McGough in *Who, Why, Where, What* (McGough, 1985). Perhaps some children do not ask questions because they feel they ought to know the answer already, or that they mustn't have been listening. They might need to be encouraged and shown how to formulate questions. Raising questions can be an important part of the beginning of work on a topic. The Walled Garden questions (which typically followed items about planning an investigation) asked:

- Is there anything else you can think of to investigate about . . . ? or
- What else would you like to find out about . . . by doing investigations?

Questions like these, as opposed to questions which *suggest* investigations, could readily be included in class discussions, or, for written assessment purposes, be part of a science worksheet which might have proposed an investigation with scope for further developments. Then, instead of all the questions being raised by the teacher or the author of the worksheet, children would be given the opportunity to raise their own. To begin with, *any* questions might be welcomed, in order to create an atmosphere in the class which is conducive to asking questions. With the teacher's encouragement, this would lead to questions of the 'how, why and what if . . .' kind (Level Two). Once this start has been made, children can be guided to express their questions in 'investigable form' (Level Four). Expressing a question in investigable form makes a considerable linguistic demand but children can only be guided towards this if they have at least asked some questions.

Interpreting

At Level Five in the National Curriculum, children should 'identify patterns', while Level Three performance involves 'generalizing'. In answering the Walled Garden items, although about half the children could discern a pattern with numerical data (LEAVES), and interpolate an appropriate number, less than 10 per cent could *describe* the pattern with a general statement. The success rate was apparently higher at Level Five than at Level Three. This raises a number of issues.

(1) Answers can be guessed with numerical data:

The number sequence { 7, 9, 10, 9, [   ], 6, 5 } was presented in a table. This was to show that the length of a holly leaf seems to depend on its position on the twig. Many of the teachers, in looking at children's responses to this question, remarked that although a child might be used to a 'fill in the missing number' type of question (for which it is possible to guess the answer), they were less used to such a question being based in a context – in this case the length of holly leaves on a twig. The context provided an opportunity for a description to be sought for the perceived pattern and this appears to have presented the greater difficulty.

(2) Data which is presented 'cold' can be difficult to comprehend:

An illustration was provided, as indeed a twig could have been. Nevertheless, children were not actively involved in the generation of the data, into which they were asked to insert a number and about which they had to write a description. Some children might quite simply not have understood the origin of the numbers and, of course, others did not have the writing skills to provide a description.

(3) The value of generating one's own data about which to generalize:

In considering the provision of opportunities for children to make progress, in interpreting, through the Levels of Attainment, it is useful to be guided by the phrase 'data from various sources' in the Level Five statement. Children's investigations might, at Level Two, enable them to 'use generalized statements' and at Level Three to 'draw conclusions' based on their own results. A higher expectation would be for children to interpret information presented to them.

An appropriate use of the products of class investigations, in encouraging children to interact with data from different sources, is to display results along with questions about what the results mean. At Level Three, for example, children 'interpret simple pictograms and bar charts', and at Level Five they 'draw conclusions from experimental results'. Some examples are provided in Chapter 8.

The practice of interpreting the results, from 'associating one factor with another' (Level Two) to describing 'patterns derived from data' (Level Five) is often difficult to encourage in the course of an investigation. A practical activity can easily take on a competitive mode. For example, the preoccupation with making the 'best floater' or the 'buggy which travels furthest' can cause the investigators to compare two results rather than look at the patterns emerging from a series of tests. There is often a need for teacher intervention to change children's reactions from 'it's the best' (i.e. better than last time) or 'it's no good' (i.e. not as good as the others') and to encourage them to focus on all the results. This can, incidentally, provide opportunities for critical reflection ('how did you go about that result?) and for considering fair testing.

Critically reflecting

Critical reflection on performance is extremely difficult to assess effectively in a written mode, for several reasons. In offering a written response there is almost certain to be a period of consideration and self-doubt which is itself a form of critical reflection. To request a child to reflect further at this point is to push the limits of co-operation. Furthermore, there is no source of further information to be turned to which might provide a fresh perspective in the written mode. In a practical situation, it is much easier to envisage alternative courses of action. The social dimension of the request is also significant, for self-criticism is more likely in a social context in which the child feels safe. The relative uncertainties of a written assessment exercise, however enjoyable or challenging, are unlikely to foster the kind of positive and immediate feedback which the interpersonal situation can offer.

The Programme of Study (Key Stage Two) states that activities in science should encourage '... evaluation against the demands of the problem'. Although not explicit in the National Curriculum Statements to Level Five, the need for constructive criticism through critical reflection is surely implicit in the 'planning' statements at Levels Four and Five (see Table 7.4). Questions such as 'was it safe?'

'was it a fair test?'

'are the results accurate?'

would begin the process. Discussion with an individual, or with groups, about their practical work and about their results can serve two purposes for the teacher:

1. Children can review critically *how* an investigation has been carried out.
2. They can look at the relevance (to the problem) and use of *what* they found out.

Planning

Children, in applying planning skills, will be deciding what they need in order to be able to carry out a particular investigation and will be identifying what is going to be measured or compared. The programmes of study for Key Stages One and Two (Science Attainment Target One) suggest, respectively, that children might 'Find a way to . . .' address an investigable question and develop the notion of a 'fair test'.

To 'identify and manipulate relevant independent and dependent variables, choosing appropriately between ranges, numbers and values' is a Level Five activity. In the STAR sample, three-quarters of children identified the need to use more than one fabric (the independent variable) in the test for waterproofness (WATER). This level of success was not reflected in all the planning questions. In the test for the favourite food of snails, about two-thirds of the children specified what they would look for (the dependent variable). So, for about half of the sample there was evidence at least once of performance at Level Five. The important feature of this level of performance is the ability to *design* an investigation. While a child might be able to follow instructions (Level Four) competently this is not necessarily an indication that the purpose of the investigation or the rationale behind its design has been understood.

Another criterion for Level Four activity is that children should be able to construct fair tests and identify and control those variables which have to be kept the same for fair comparisons to be made. In the context of the Walled Garden material, the judgement was made that children could be expected to identify up to three controls in their plans for an investigation. This is an arbitrary judgement. Children who do manage to control three variables can certainly be deemed to have got the idea. To ask for three also allows some latitude in discounting some suggestions which are wide of the mark. It does seem that, once they've got hold of the idea, some children get into the mould of 'control everything', including the colour of the pullover to be worn during the investigation! Nearly three-quarters of the children who completed the questions in WATER, WALLS and MINIBEASTS were able to identify at least one variable which needed to be controlled for fairness.

What might these findings mean for classroom practice? It is clear that children need opportunities to plan their own investigations, to share their plans and to put them into practice. The following examples are based on the criteria developed for the assessment of children's performance in the STAR project practical task (see Russell and Harlen, 1990), and form useful bases on which to evaluate the provision being made for children in school.

1. Do the children apply their own ideas?

One boy, who was pursuing an investigation which *he* had designed, to answer a question which the whole class had addressed, was asked by the teacher what he thought of 'this way of working . . .?' (putting his plan into action, instead of following instructions as had been his previous experience). He said that he thought it was good because he felt that the work was 'his'! It is always worth asking oneself 'Whose question is it anyway?' in order to try to avoid the experience of one teacher whose children said, at the start of a practical session 'Oh no, not another problem, sir!'

2. Do the children identify relevant starting points for investigations?

Often, the novelty of a situation distracts from the investigation. Using the example of snails' food preference, if children are not used to using hand lenses, close observation of the details of the way in which a snail consumes food might result in a variety of scraps being offered to the snail with no concern for how to judge apparent preference.

3. Do children perform fair tests and quantify outcomes?

Children need to be taught to identify a relevant variable to change or compare and then to identify a variable to measure. A group of third-year girls was investigating fabrics and decided to look for signs of shrinkage in water. Although they selected a variety of different threads to test, they gave no thought as to how to measure the outcome. After carefully controlling for time and temperature, they had no quantified outcome to report!

Although one way of practising the development of planning skills would be to *write down* detailed plans prior to every investigation, it is important to note that this is not always desirable. A verbal report or a discussion in which a number of alternative proposals are considered, or indeed a description dictated into a tape recorder (which one group elected to do after observing the teacher using the machine for a similar purpose himself!) would all help the teacher to judge a child's attainment. A number of the National Curriculum Statements of Attainment begin with the word 'describe . . .', which implies a spoken just as much as a written description. Indeed, in one class, the teacher always insisted on careful plans being drawn up and committed to paper before an investigation, and reported that the children's performance in planning was excellent. Then came the discovery that *practice* did not often match *plan*! It seemed that the process of compiling a detailed plan had become more ritualistic than meaningful.

Recording

Since written assessment is limited in terms of opportunities for *collecting* actual data, there are two main devices that may be employed as a substitute. The first is to use the closely related skill of *reading* data; this will help to locate any areas of specific difficulty. The other strategy which may be employed is to ask children to transpose data from one form to another. In doing so, they will reveal their understanding of the rules governing the construction and use of co-ordinate forms. Appropriate forms of recording include tables, bar charts and line graphs. Tables may summarize information in one or more of a number of modes: symbolic, pictorial, verbal or numerical, or any combination of these.

The questions in the Walled Garden material required performance equivalent to National Curriculum Level Five (describing patterns in presented data – LEAVES, WALLS), Level Four (constructing a block graph – WALLS; completing a table – SUN-DIAL) and at Level Two (listing observations – LEAVES). Eight out of ten children satisfied the Level Two criterion; nearly three-quarters achieved Level Four and only 5 per cent successfully made a 'written statement of the pattern derived from . . . data'. These aspects of performance in science can reflect skills formally learned in mathematics. Children's performance in recording often disappointed teachers. One reflected:

> were the children simply not transferring their mathematical knowledge to science, or do they really not understand the concepts of graphs?

Other comments included:

> interpretation of the graph was very disappointing as they have all done similar work

> reading from a graph caused far more problems . . . a heavy concentration in the past on reading from and recording in only one format – the table?

A number of deficiencies in children's performance were apparent when their responses were compared with the STAR criteria for success. Opportunities need to be provided for children to improve such performance. In order to do so, teachers might find it useful to answer the following questions:

- Do I ask for results to be reported as line graphs as well as bar charts and block graphs?
- Can the children label the axes of a graph?
- Are the children consistent with their use of units in recording numerical data?

The Programmes of Study for Science Attainment Target One also include the *reporting* aspects of recording as being important. Teachers need to give children opportunities to decide the appropriate method of recording and to generate incentives for reporting by extending the audience to whom investigations are reported. A variety of forms of pictorial, graphical, and tabular records, structured notes and photographs can, in combination form a report. The report needs a heading or a title: this must convey the meaning of the information. Numerical data needs consistency in units and tabular presentation requires careful labelling. Ways of highlighting the importance of consistency and care are as follows:

- Several groups perform similar investigations and collect data and compare results. The results will have meaning only if the use of units of measure is consistent.
- The class as a whole works in groups and enters data on a chart or a database. Categories under which data is collated need careful labelling to avoid confusion.

Measuring

Measurement is so indisputably a practical activity that there is little point in distorting a written assessment to accommodate it.

The National Curriculum criteria refer to measuring instruments. In the one question (SUN-DIAL) where children were asked to use a ruler, two-thirds were found to be at Level Three (quantify to the nearest labelled division). Much of children's ability to measure will be recorded by teachers as achievement in mathematics (Attainment Target Eight). For example, in the LEAVES question, areas were calculated using squared paper.

Significant for Attainment Target One in science is the wording (Levels Three, Four and Five) '*select* and use . . .'. This emphasis on practical performance (equally important in the Mathematics Attainment Targets One and Nine: 'Using and applying mathematics') is difficult to assess on paper. However, in assessing children's plans for investigations (WATER, WALLS, MINIBEASTS, BARK) the criterion '*quantification* of the dependent variable' was applied. A distinction needs to be made between quantifying a problem and being able to measure. Overall, less than one-tenth of children suggested measuring any outcome – although in these cases the measurement would not necessarily require the use of a measuring instrument. For the children who didn't suggest any quantification in their investigations, it would not be true to infer that they are unable to measure accurately. The significant difference is between knowing *how* and knowing *why* or *when* to measure. As a result of assessing their children's responses, some teachers were surprised at the apparent inability to transfer skills:

> I found it interesting that children I knew to be of a fairly high standard found it difficult to transfer skills learnt in maths to science.

The implication for teaching is, as in recording, to extend the opportunities provided by exercises in planning, by asking questions such as:

> 'Why are you going to measure or compare?'

> 'How are you going to measure it/them?'

(remembering that *consistency* in measurement is important and is possibly more appropriate than the use of standard units).

8

Developing and assessing process skills

In this chapter we look at how teachers can use written assessment procedures to help in judging children's levels of attainment in science. Two points must first be stressed:

1. Written assessment is appropriate only for certain aspects of attainment; for others there must be 'live' assessment of children engaged in science tasks;
2. The fact that written work is to be assessed does not necessarily preclude practical activity.

This chapter is as much about the assessment of *any* written product of children's science activities as about the development of materials specifically designed for written assessment. In both cases, the crucial factor is that the child's response will be compared with some predetermined criterion describing a particular process skill in terms of what a child should be able to do or have done. As the TGAT report (DES, 1988) suggested, children need not even be aware that they are being assessed, whether by Standard Assessment Tasks (SATs) or as part of the teacher-based assessment which is needed to inform teaching provision throughout each key stage.

Written assessment depends, of course, on children's reading and writing skills to a large extent, and this makes the advantages of this form of assessment less accessible to teachers of infant-age children. Later in this chapter, some strategies for overcoming this problem will be outlined.

Although opportunities to demonstrate some of the eight process skills were rarely incorporated into the science activities we observed in the classrooms of STAR teachers, many children *could* demonstrate them, *when given the opportunity*, as shown in Chapter 7. A distinct advantage of written assessment is that it gives every child, individually, the opportunity to demonstrate his or her skills. While written tasks are difficult for some children because of their dependence on literacy skills, practical situations and discussion tasks depend heavily on social skills, personality and self-confidence, especially in group work. In other words, for a 'fair test' of children's performance, both forms of assessment are needed.   *Relate to Daniel's work*

WRITTEN ASSESSMENT IN THE CLASSROOM

In this section we look at how those process skills which children were rarely seen to demonstrate (hypothesizing and raising questions, for example) might be incorporated into class activities and how the teacher can obtain written evidence of the children's performance in these skills.

In the visits to classrooms during the STAR project, we found that children had plenty of opportunity to practise the skills of planning investigations and making observations but that some of the other skills were rarely used. The worksheets and tasks prepared by the STAR teachers usually encouraged planning, observing, recording and measuring but rarely required any hypothesizing, interpreting of data, raising questions for investigation or critical reflection. These might be regarded as higher-order skills in the sense that interpretation cannot be made, for example, unless some data has been collected first; likewise, observations of puzzling phenomena or conflicting events can be used to stimulate children to form hypotheses; critical reflection cannot be carried out without an investigation to reflect upon. For the Walled Garden material, investigations and results had to be 'manufactured' but in the course of class science, procedures and data will arise naturally from the children's activities.

Raising questions

A quick look at many a contemporary science workcard reveals a plethora of questions, many of which suggest investigations for children to try. Tasks set in science sessions which require children to 'carry out an investigation to find out . . .' do not give children themselves much opportunity to raise their own questions or to pursue what they would like to find out. In other words, questions for investigation are usually raised *for* the children *by* the teacher (or authors of the science scheme).

For example, each group in a class of seven-year-olds was given pieces of several different fabrics to observe (to feel, smell, stretch, crumple and listen to, as well as to look at). The children were then encouraged to express their observations about some of the fabrics as questions. Once they had been shown *how* to 'convert' their observations:

'this one's rough';

'this one's shiny';

'this is like elastic',

into questions:

'is it smooth?'

'is it shiny?'

'does it stretch?'

each group produced at least four questions to apply to some other pieces of fabric. By limiting the number of questions required from each group, the teacher made the task manageable and obtained a written record because the children wrote down their questions in a list for a table of observations. This task could readily have become a written assessment task which formed a natural part of the children's science activities. The teacher could have specified beforehand a basic criterion that the children should, as step one, ask *any* question. The next stage, and the next criterion level, might be to see if the children could produce *one* 'what will happen if . . .?' question (Level 2; see Table 7.4, p. 76) such as, in the fabrics example:

'what will happen if I stretch/screw up and let go/wet/pull a thread of this fabric?'

or

'how far will this leg-of-a-pair-of tights stretch and what will happen if/when I let go?'

One of the criteria for Level Four performance is that children can 'raise a question in investigable form'. Once a child has shown that s/he can raise questions of any kind, questions for investigation can be encouraged in classwork. It might follow directly from the interpretation of a table of observations. For example:

'Is this kind of fabric more stretchy than that kind?'

This satisfies the criterion that the question must require an investigation.

The Level Five criteria in Attainment Target One include the statement that children can 'use concepts, knowledge and skills to suggest simple questions and design investigations to answer them'. In other words, children are expected to incorporate some form of hypothesis into the question. When asked to think of

'one thing you could investigate about fabrics'

or

'an investigation to do using these fabrics'

some children wrote

> 'are knitted fabrics stretchier than woven ones?'

or

> 'do loosely woven fabrics let water through more quickly than tightly woven ones?'

These children have applied either their observations, interpretations and hypotheses or their knowledge of fabrics and have raised a question for investigation which begins to meet the Level Five criterion.

None of the teacher intervention described above is to suggest that major attention is being applied to assessment. The questions can all be a natural part of science activities or be added to worksheets. If the children write down their answers individually as part of the record of the activity on that occasion, the teacher will then have samples of the children's question-raising skills to take away and sort into groups such as the following:

(a) no questions at all;
(b) simple observation questions;
(c) questions for investigation.

The teacher will then be able to see what point in question-raising the children have reached and where to target general work on question-raising. If most of the children raised the same kind of question they might need help in formulating questions or in developing them into investigable ones. At the same time, the work described above would have contributed to Science Attainment Target Six (Types and uses of materials). The teacher could also make judgements about which Statements of Attainment had been met by the outcomes of the task and go on to decide which aspects of understanding and knowledge to plan for next.

Interpreting observations and data

The skill of interpreting presupposes that a set of data has been made or recorded, which may or may not be in tabular or graphical form. In the STAR project class observations, we found that children were often engaged in making observations and sometimes in measuring, and that they made recordings in a table. It was relatively rare, however, for children to have the opportunity to interpret their findings by looking for patterns in the set of measurements or observations. Even when they had collected and tabulated a set of results, it often required teacher intervention to encourage children to survey the *full* set of results. In a written task or instruction, this sort of encouragement can be written in and the children's attention can be drawn to the idea that there might be a pattern in the results.

In a task similar to the fabrics example, a class was examining a range of materials including various metals. The questions they raised included:

'does it bend?'

'does it feel cold?'

'is it shiny?'

'does it conduct electricity?'

The questions were written down the side of the page, one question for each row of a grid. The name of one of the materials was written at the head of each column. The children answered the questions by putting a tick or a cross in the appropriate box. Many teachers used this tabular format for recording observations for other topics such as leaves, papers, balls and potatoes. In the first place they decided to work on the skills of making observations, of measuring and of recording results. Once the results were recorded, the children could be lead (if they didn't make the moves themselves!) to interpret their findings by looking for associations of one factor and another (a Level Two criterion) or by drawing conclusions from their results (Level Four). A few questions, devised after the tables or charts of observations had been compiled, encouraged the children to make interpretations based on their data.

The observations of class activity in the STAR project and the written assessments suggest that many children can see such patterns *when they are asked to look for them*, but that during science activities they tend to look back only to the previous measurement and to attempt interpretations based on only part of the data.

When the children have had an opportunity to understand what is required of them, they can be asked to write down their own interpretations as an extension to an observation exercise thus providing the teacher with a form of evidence on which they can reflect afterwards. What sorts of question could be used to encourage interpretation? Returning to the examples above, the questions could be very general, such as:

'Can you see any patterns in the table of results?'

It might prove necessary to direct children to certain factors to compare. Studies of younger children's visual search skills suggest that they do not carry out the systematic 'point-by-point' search typical of an older child or an adult but, after a quick random scan, might fixate on one similar feature in two arrays and generalize from this to conclude overall similarity (Wood, 1988). The teacher has a clear role here, to teach children to look for patterns by providing structured opportunities for children to practise studying a table or a chart. More specific questions directing attention to particular features might be needed. For example:

'Is there anything else the same about all the ones that feel cold?'

Or

'Find out which ones were shiny. Do the shiny ones also feel cold/conduct electricity/bend? Explain how you decided the answer.'

In these cases, too, the written responses could also be used as evidence of achievement in Attainment Targets Six (Types and uses of materials) and Eleven (Electricity and magnetism). In another class where the focus was on making observations and on measuring, the task was to compare three potatoes. The observations and measurements to be made were written down the side of the grid, for example:

'length (cm)'

'shortest circumference ('waist' measurement) (cm)'

'weight (g)'

'how many "eyes"?'

'does it feel smooth or rough?'

Once again, the addition of some extra questions could be provided to extend an observation activity into an interpretation opportunity, by turning attention to the whole table of results. For example:

'Are fatter potatoes heavier?'

'Do the longest potatoes have more eyes?'

'Is there a pattern in the lengths and weights?'

A general question 'Can you see any patterns (trends) in your results?' could be asked. Such questions might be asked in a plenary session at the end of the lesson or in a short 'review' session the next day. The teacher could collate the class results for, say, weight and 'waist' and the children could plot one against the other. Alternatively, they could try to grade the potatoes by circumference (or by any other recorded attribute). The children could decide the limits for each 'grade' or class and consider how easy it is to judge or how quickly they can determine the circumference. By systematically collecting and tabulating evidence collected about class performance, as some STAR teachers did with their Walled Garden results, the teacher's own skills of interpretation could be applied. This helps in looking at the pattern across the whole class. Which of the teacher's criteria have been met?

- Could most children plot a histogram?
- Were those who could plot a histogram able to draw (and/or express satisfactorily) a conclusion from it?

- Did the response show that a child could associate one factor with another? (Level Two).
- Could the child make a generalized statement based on his or her observations? (Level Three).
- Did the child identify a pattern in the data? (Level Five).
- Does the class as a whole need more practice in plotting line graphs?
- Which children need to work on the presentation of tables so that they have a chance of discerning a pattern?!

Just as children often draw conclusions on the basis of one or two observations, so there is a danger, without some systematic observation and recording of the performance of each child, or at least of an adequate sample of children, that the teacher might form a generalized impression about the performance of the whole class, based on the outstanding contributions of one or two children. While class discussion is an important vehicle for teaching, by sharing interpretations, for example, and for children to learn from each other, one or two responses indicating a high level of attainment could create a false impression – hence the importance of written, whole-class assessment from time to time.

For a written assessment of children's levels of attainment in interpreting data, some questions could be used as part of a science activity. There would be no need to assess all the other process skills at the same time; neither would it be necessary to prepare a full assessment project or to insist on test conditions, although it might be useful to let the children know that the teacher was 'interested in each individual's ideas' and that 'there could be a variety of different answers to the problem'.

Hypothesizing

In Chapter 7, we reported that about three-quarters of the children who tried the Walled Garden tasks, were able to suggest a reasonable hypothesis to explain why two children could not find any snails in a garden where other minibeasts lived. Our observations and individual practical assessment task as part of the STAR project showed that the vast majority of children, including five-year-olds, could suggest reasonable hypotheses to explain events, when given the opportunity. In the classroom observation, hypothesizing was rarely observed in the course of classroom activities and, when it was, it usually happened when there was teacher involvement. This presented two problems: first, how to get children to hypothesize more and, second, how to get them to do so independently of the teacher.

In the STAR project, the criterion for recording a hypothesis was that a child used his or her science knowledge or introduced some conceptual basis to explain a phenomenon. In the National Curriculum for Science, the criteria for Level Three performance include the statement that the child can 'formulate hypotheses', and for Level Four can 'formulate testable hypotheses'. No conceptual basis is specified, but for attainment at Level Five, hypothesizing on the basis of science concepts is included in the statement which requires children to 'use concepts, knowledge and skills to suggest simple questions and design investigations to answer them'. Unfortunately, perhaps the same influence which seems to prevent children raising questions in school prevents them, consequently, from seeking explanations. How can this influence be counteracted?

In order to increase children's confidence to offer hypotheses in class review or discussion times, the STAR teachers tried to develop strategies to create a more 'accepting' class atmosphere. In fact, this general approach was necessary for critical reflection, too. As explained in Chapter 7, the children must be confident that the teacher will not disapprove, disregard or reject their ideas, but also that it is not detrimental to reject or criticize their own ideas. This confidence took time to develop. In our observations, the two following aspects seemed to characterize situations in which children felt free to hypothesize in the teacher's presence (usually in a class plenary):

(a) a feeling of *having time*, of slowing down the usual rapid pace of classroom interaction; of the teacher waiting long enough to allow children time to think and to collect up the words to express difficult ideas;
(b) the other was the use of the teaching skill of *accepting children's ideas* without, unintentionally but by force of habit, 'correcting' them before the children themselves have a chance to test or evaluate the ideas. If children have confidence to express their ideas in class, they might be even more ready to commit them to paper, particularly when they don't have to 'compete' for a turn to speak, as in a class discussion.

This has digressed some way from the subject of incorporating written tasks which can be used for assessment, but it might be through the inclusion of certain kinds of questions in the presentation of activities that children, working in groups, can be encouraged to formulate hypotheses without teacher intervention. What sorts of questions or instructions can be used to get children to hypothesize and how can they be included in everyday science?

In the Walled Garden material, invitations to hypothesize always followed some observation or investigation which provided some event for the children to try to explain. The children were then asked,

'Can you think of any reasons why . . .?'

'What do you think might have been a reason for . . . the results you have obtained . . .'

'Can you suggest one reason for the . . . needle floating on the water, the paper gyro spinning as it floats to the ground . . . the red ball bouncing higher than the others . . .?'

'Could there be any other possible reasons?'

The question format itself is simple enough, and yet such questions were rarely included in the worksheets that the teachers prepared or used. If questions like these were added to worksheets in group-work settings, or put to the whole class after carrying out an investigation, making observations, and perhaps interpreting their results, and the children were to include their ideas in their record of the activity, then the teacher would have written evidence on which to base a judgement of the child's level of attainment in hypothesizing. What criteria would be used to assess a child's answer?

In one class, the children were doing a chromatography task, from a worksheet. They were asked to record their observations, and to try different inks, but they were not asked, on the worksheet, to think about where the colours came from or why the 'blot' on the paper contained colours, rather than staying black, or gradually fading through the greys. Suppose they had been, how would the teacher assess their ideas? The following are some 'invented' ideas:

1. 'It's to do with the way the water spreads the ink out.'
2. 'It's the colours in the paper.'
3. 'The water carries the colours in the ink.'
4. 'Is it because some of the ink powders are heavier than others?'
5. 'It's like when rain makes a rainbow.'
6. 'The ink dissolves in the water and then the paper soaks up the water and the colours get stuck on the paper.'

Every one of these ideas could be regarded as a 'reasonable' hypothesis, although the teacher might want to probe further in the rainbow one, for example. In every other case, the child has mentioned some relevant feature of the situation, so all would meet the Level Three criterion (formulate hypotheses). At Level Four, the ideas need to be testable. For this, the child would need to be asked how s/he could test the idea, and this might lead to the brink of question-raising, of the kind indicated in the Level Five Statement of Attainment. For example, the hypotheses 1, 3 and 6 above might be tested by trying chromatography with milk, spirit or washing-up liquid; idea 2 could lead to the use of different types of paper; ideas 4 and 6 go further still, to bring in a mechanism for what is happening, and concepts to explain why: the effects of gravity on the ink's constituents; the idea that ink *has* constituents, and the combination of the effects of solubility and absorbency. By being asked 'How could you test these ideas?' the children could be encouraged to show that they can demonstrate higher levels of performance – but only if they have had the chance to show their ideas in the first place.

Critically reflecting

Various significant considerations were put forward in Chapter 7 which limit the advisability of trying to assess critical reflection through the written mode. In practical work, on the other hand, when children have designed their investigations themselves, or carried out investigations proposed by the teacher, more opportunities for critical reflection will arise. Critical reflection was often observed as part of the planning process, as children revised their plans part way through an investigation but, in order to learn from these spontaneous corrections, perhaps some review session would be useful after the activities are finished. The review could take the form of a class discussion in which the children relate and discuss each other's approaches and evaluate their own approach to the problem, provided that this can be achieved with positive (i.e. 'what we have learned from this') outcomes.

In an attempt at written assessment of this skill, children might, however, be encouraged by a series of questions to evaluate various features of their investigations. For example, children might be asked to complete a report on an investigation and to include:

'. . . ways in which the investigation could be made better, fairer . . .'

'how you would carry out this investigation if you had to do it again?'

'. . . whether your test was fair? Write down how you know.'

The suggestions show that by modifying or extending present practice, by including certain types of question, which 'target' certain skills as part of science worksheets, or activities which include a written record, teachers can obtain written evidence to support their judgements of children's performance levels. The most important aspect of this formative type of assessment is that of knowing what criterion to use to assess a child's response. This chapter and the preceding one have tried to show how the National Curriculum Statements of Attainment for Attainment Target One can be used for this purpose. By 'taking away' children's written responses in order to examine them away from the demands of the classroom, the teacher can get an overview of the performance of the class in any particular skill and topic area. Although time-consuming, the discovery that, for example, few of the children raised any questions at all, will give a more useful direction to future teaching. Equally, the awareness that, while three or four children working collaboratively could plan a fair test, controlling the relevant variables, the majority could not do this on their own, or during advance planning, provides guidance on the areas for future teaching and intervention.

WRITTEN ASSESSMENT MATERIALS AND KEY STAGE ONE CHILDREN

Clearly, written assessment materials such as the Walled Garden, which was originally prepared with nine- to eleven-year-olds in mind, are not suitable for most five- to seven-year-olds. This does not have to mean, however, that infant teachers must rely completely on on-the-spot assessment and observation, although these methods will, of course, play a much larger part in assessment in these ages. Every teacher has to balance the importance of children recording their science activities against the negative effects of anxiety about, or the laboriousness of, writing for some children. Some early-years' teachers will feel that the assessment of young children's science skills through their written work will have relatively little validity because there is such a chasm between what young children can express when talking and what they can write. The suggestions made here are certainly not intended to imply that the written mode is the most appropriate for young children – it obviously is not! On the other hand, some representational record, whether written, drawn, spoken, acted out or sculpted, which can be used to 'carry' the children's ideas, questions and discoveries out of their immediate context, will be of value. Indeed, the acquisition of the skills needed to make these conversions from real to reported form is a major underlying aim of much early-years' education, although the written word may not be the chosen medium: it could be the composition of a number sentence $(3 + 5 = 8)$ to show that where there were three things there are now eight, or of some music, utilizing classroom junk 'instruments', to represent the way minibeasts move.

Although most of the assessment of younger children's science attainment will be on-the-spot assessment, infant teachers will still need 'take-away' evidence to enable them to get an overview of attainment levels in the class, and to help in their planning. In other words, the skills involved in reporting can legitimately be used in science provided that they play a minor role compared with practical activity and the sharing of ideas through talk. So bearing these things in mind, how can records be made and 'take-away' evidence of science skills be obtained from first-school children?

The importance of having a purpose   *relate to Sabrina's*

The importance of the context in which young children are operating has been recognized (e.g. Donaldson, 1978). To have a genuine purpose for one's activity can help everyone to perform more effectively, but perhaps this has greatest significance in the early years. A selection of such purposes, which must of course be shared with the children, might be as follows:

- to share the children's ideas with another class or another teacher;

- to teach parents or grandparents about science – work could be prepared for an open 'science evening';
- to put ideas forward for the whole class in deciding which plan(s) to use or what to look for;
- to communicate discoveries to a newspaper, (national, local or class-based), the children being reporters or journalists; this would limit the space available for writing . . .;
- to collect information for a mock television programme like 'Tomorrow's World', with a made-up title . . . 'Wildlife on the Football Field', 'Science at Six'. The children could be researchers or presenters, or be interviewed as experts;
- to send information back to headquarters if the children were explorers – on another planet, or in another place . . .;
- to write letters of complaint or protest to manufacturers or advertisers;

or even just because the teacher wants to find out about *everyone's* ideas.

Talking, reporting and recording: what is the difference?

Attainment Target One suggests that children should be able, at Level One to:

describe and communicate their observations, ideally through talking . . .

It is important to distinguish here what we mean by talking, reporting and recording.

- 'Talk' refers to dialogue which involves children as they carry out activities.
- 'Reporting' refers to spoken accounts of observations and ideas which may be offered during a class discussion after some practical activities or when the teacher asks, 'What can you remember about what we found out yesterday . . . ?', or when the teacher asks individuals, or a group, 'How are you getting on?' or 'What are you trying to do now?'
- 'Recording' is one of the process skills used in the STAR project to refer to children talking about, or actually making a record of, any aspect of the science process as a whole. The record might be written, pictorial, graphical or numerical, or taped, photographed, filmed, word-processed or a set of exhibits. Our main concern here is with the children's ability to use this skill to reveal their use of the other skills.

When children are simply talking about science activities, or reporting them, then it will be the teacher who does the recording, and this might be longhand on paper, by putting ticks on a checklist of skills or comments that the teacher is hoping will emerge, or by tape recorder or video camera.

WHAT FORMS OF RECORD WOULD MAKE USEFUL 'TAKE-AWAY' EVIDENCE?

To refer again to Level One of Attainment Target One, the teacher will want to listen in on children's active observation-making, and might note who in the group actually made any observations but not what they said. On the other hand the teacher might write down that one child said, 'Look, these two seeds have both got a groove down one side,' or that no one remarked on the shape of the seeds until s/he had intervened, 'Has anybody noticed anything about the shapes of these seeds?' She might 'tick' these skills as on a checklist, or decide to write them down longhand for discussion with the children later.

Tape recording

The tape recorder provides one way to 'capture' children's verbal reports. The children, in a small group, could be asked to think of THREE things to say about how the seeds are like each other, or how they are different from each other. When they have decided, as a group, which three things to say, they could record their statements on a cassette to be played to the class later. They might be asked to think of ONE thing to say about the seeds' sizes, about their colours, about the patterns on them and about what they feel like to hold. Either the tape itself, or a note of its contents and speakers, then becomes the record of the children's skills and can be used as take-away evidence for assessment purposes. The children will still have had to formulate reports of their ideas, but will be saved the labour of writing them down.

Drawing

Drawing is probably the most common 'written' form of communication used by younger children. It can be used to provide evidence of visual observations. The children could be given sheets ruled into 'boxes' for them to show what they have noticed. Plans for investigations, of methods to be used, can also be drawn, as they were for the 'snails' investigations in the Walled Garden question. Hypotheses can often be illustrated with the addition of well-placed arrows, and a few words or labels. Teachers often 'annotate' the children's drawings while talking to the children so that, later, the teacher can remember what the child was trying to draw. Modifications to designs can be shown by asking for a drawing of the original and then a drawing of the modification. One teacher who used this technique was then able to 'glean' the children's predictive hypotheses about what they thought would make a parachute into a better parachute: some used a different shape, some put more holes in the 'canvas'; some stuck feathers to it; some planned to fray the edges . . . and so on. Not all the children were able to make their plans clear, but the teacher was able to ask the children to explain, and offered to write labels for them if they needed help at that stage. This set of predictions was then available for comparison with the results.

Writing

How can the task of writing be eased, minimized or made attractive for those children who do not particularly relish it? Given a *real* purpose for writing:

1. The teacher could write the children's words, just as is common practice after recording their stories or picture titles.
2. The writing could be shared among the members of a group or between partners. The group might choose 'the best writer' or take it in turns to record the group's ideas.
3. Very simple worksheets *can* be devised. In one class, children working in pairs wrote down, in a few words, their observations of 'what happened when . . . ?' and their hypotheses after carrying out an investigation. The children recorded what happened by a series of drawings and either chose a 'good writer' to write down their answers to 'What do you think was happening inside the . . . ?', or took it in turns to write. Later in the day, the children came to sit in the 'carpet corner' to discuss the results. The teacher used the groups' record sheets to get the children to elaborate and share their observations and hypotheses: she would take two sheets and say, for example, 'Now Claire's group noticed that . . . , but in Simon's group . . .'. After the observations had been discussed, she asked what the children thought was happening, and again referred to the record sheets: 'Someone in Alison's group had the idea that . . . . Can you tell everyone about it . . . ?' By holding the groups' record sheets in her hand and going through them with the children sitting around her, the children were reminded of their ideas and could elaborate and share (and communicate) them. Their interest was held, as they hoped that their sheet would be next (this teacher was not only accepting but intrinsically valued all the ideas enough to discuss them). Afterwards the teacher not only had 'take-away' evidence on which to ascertain the range of attainment levels in the class for the skills in National Curriculum Science Attainment Target One, but she had had the opportunity to probe the more cryptic statements and seek elaborations where necessary.
4. Finally, there is the ploy of using media other than pencil and paper; the children might be encouraged to write their observations, or questions raised, with the fat felt-tip pens which teachers use, on cards cut to size to be displayed; the old-fashioned equivalent of this would be to use chalk and the blackboard (if one can be found!).

Epilogue

The rationale for this book is based on the value for teachers of knowing about the levels of achievement, in the science process skills, of the children in their classes. We have discussed such levels of achievement both in terms of the STAR project and as they are described by the National Curriculum Science Attainment Target One. Our purpose was not only to describe what children *can* do, but also to offer suggestions and to share ideas about what teachers might do to build on the present achievement of children. While we have focused on assessment through the media of writing and drawing, many of the points which have been made apply to all assessments, in whatever way they are carried out.

This information can be useful only in so far as we have some idea of progress in both the skills and the knowledge of science so that we can help children along both these paths. In other words, knowing what a child has achieved is no use unless we know the direction and nature of progress from that point. The National Curriculum has provided a description of progression in terms of 'Levels of Attainment' towards 'Attainment Targets'. This progression is based on current experience and research, but is *not* 'written in stone'. Who knows what might happen with vastly increased experience of teaching and learning in science in the primary school; children may make much more rapid, and possibly differently directed, progress in future years. It is important, therefore, that teachers constantly review not only the progress that children are able to make, but also the ways in which that progress is facilitated, described and assessed.

The 'critical reflection' which we have advocated for children with regard to their investigations is equally applicable to teachers with regard to their teaching and to the assessment of children's progress. Teachers will be able to make a significant contribution when the time for revision of the National Curriculum and of the assessment procedures arrives, as a consequence of systematic observation and recording of children's progress, and the consequent accumulation of evidence of what children can do and of the progress they can make.

Appendix I: Walled Garden Worksheets

Name .... Date of birth ....

Bark Rubbings

sweet chesnut

ash

holly

oak

hornbeam

silver birch

All these rubbings are life-size and the right way up

The project folder explains how bark rubbings are made. Make your own bark rubbing.

If you cannot find any bark, make a rubbing of a brick wall, or the floor, or some other surface.

Do this before you answer the questions.

1. On which of the trees would you be able to feel ridges going <u>round</u> the trunk?

....

....

....

2. Which of the trees would have deep spaces in the bark that you could get a finger into?

....

....

....

3. Which of the trees would have a bark feeling like this?
    "Fairly even surface. No large holes or ridges.
    Many small spots or bumps sticking up."

....

....

....

4. Insects can be found in the deep slits and cracks in bark. Birds that eat insects search the bark with their long thin beaks. Look at the bark rubbings and choose <u>four</u> on which you might expect to find birds catching insects.

    1 ....

    2 ....

    3 ....

    4 ....

5. Describe how the bark of the oak tree would feel.

    ....

    ....

    ....

    ....

    ....

6.   What would you do to find out whether the bark on a
     tree's trunk changes from year to year?

....

....

....

....

....

Name .... Date of birth ....

Leaves

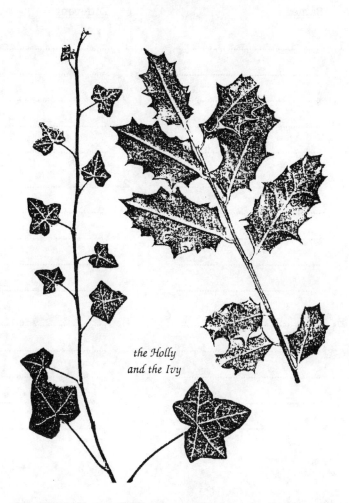

the Holly
and the Ivy

Sue, Nicky, Vince and Eddie saw a holly tree and some ivy covering a wall near to it. They carefully picked one leaf from each and compared them.

Look at a <u>real</u> holly leaf and a <u>real</u> ivy leaf.

1.   Look for three ways in which they are the same, and three
     ways in which they are different.

Same	Different
1.	1. ....
....	....
....	....
....	....
....	....
2.	2. ....
....	....
....	....
....	....
....	....
3.	3. ....
....	....
....	....
....	....
....	....

2. Nicky and Vince noticed that there were lots of different sized leaves in the ivy growing up the garden wall. They asked everyone in their group to pick a leaf. Back at school they drew round their leaves on squared paper to find the area of each leaf.

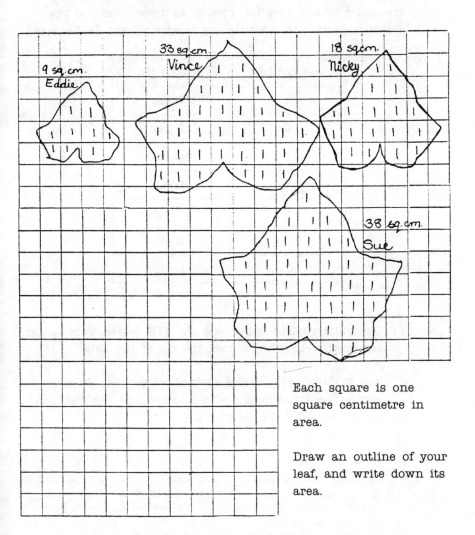

Each square is one square centimetre in area.

Draw an outline of your leaf, and write down its area.

Sue wondered, "Are holly leaves different sizes?"

They asked their teacher to cut a holly twig for them. There is a picture of it in the project folder.

The holly leaves were too prickly to draw round so the children decided to measure the length of each leaf instead.

leaf position	leaf length
1	7 cm
2	9 cm
3	10 cm
4	9 cm
5	cm
6	6 cm
7	5 cm

3. a) The children had found that the IVY leaves were larger the further they were from the tip of the twig.

   Are HOLLY leaves arranged that way? What do you notice about the length of the leaves and the distance from the tip of the twig?

   ....

   ....

   ....

   b) What do you <u>think</u> the length of leaf 5 might have been? .... cm. (The picture is NOT the right size.)

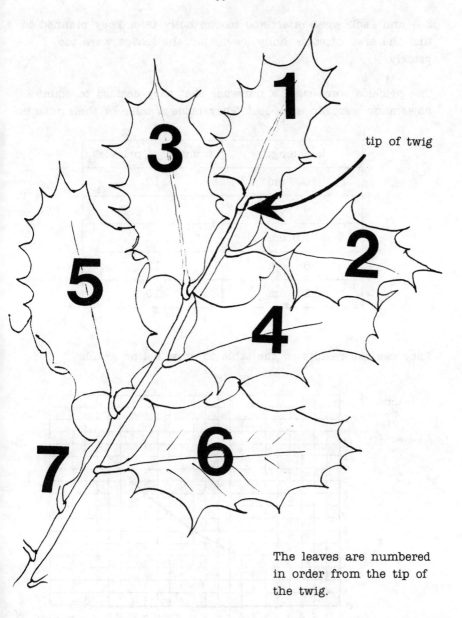

tip of twig

The leaves are numbered
in order from the tip of
the twig.

Sue and Jack were interested in the holly tree. They planned to find the area of some holly leaves but the leaves were too prickly.

The prickles were such a nuisance that they decided to count how many were on each leaf. They made a table of their results.

leaf length	number of prickles
10 cm	17
9 cm	16
7.5 cm	14
6 cm	12
5 cm	10

They use the results in the table to draw a line graph.

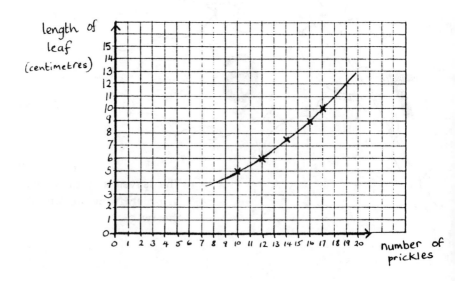

4. How many prickles do you think there would be on a leaf 12 cm long? ....

    How did you decide your answer?

    ....

    ....

    ....

    ....

5. The children made two discoveries. The first was:

    Holly leaves do not all have the same number of prickles.

    See if you can work out the second discovery. It is about leaf lengths and prickle numbers. Write it down.

    ....

    ....

    ....

    ....

Name .... Date of birth ....

Minibeasts

Dan and Tammy kept a note of all the "minibeasts" they found in the Walled Garden. They drew the minibeasts as well as they could.

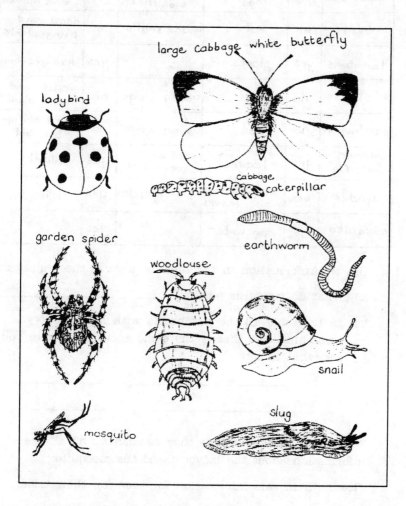

large cabbage white butterfly

ladybird

cabbage caterpillar

garden spider

woodlouse

earthworm

snail

mosquito

slug

Read about the "minibeasts" in the project folder before you try to answer the questions.

Later, back at school, they used some books to get
information about the minibeasts. They made a special
chart, called a table, which showed the information and put
it in the Walled Garden project folder. Here is a copy of it.

Minibeast	legs	where eggs laid	eggs hatch into	sheds skin	adult feeds on
woodlouse	yes	under stones, logs	young woodlice	yes	dead animals and plants
snail	no	soil	young snails	no	dead and living plants
ladybird	yes	plants		yes	live greenfly
slug	no	soil	young slugs	no	dead and living plants
earthworm	no	soil	young worms	no	dead things in the soil
cabbage butterfly	yes	leaves	larva caterpillar	yes	plants
spider	yes	in cocoon on leaves	young spiders	yes	flies
mosquito	yes	on water		yes	

1. Use the information in the table to answer these questions:

    a) What do ladybirds feed on? ....

    b) In the table all the minibeasts with legs have
        something else that is the same about them. Can you
        see what it is?

        ....

        ....

2. When they made the table they could not find all the
    information about the ladybird and the mosquito.

    Please fill in this information for them on their table:

    a) A ladybird's egg hatches into a LARVA.

    b) Adult mosquitos feed on ANIMALS and PLANTS.

3. Dan and Tammy's table shows that snails eat dead and living plants, but it doesn't say whether they like to eat some plants more than others.

Suppose you have these foods that snails will eat:

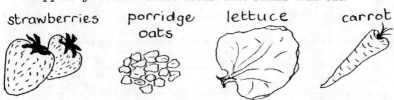

strawberries   porridge   lettuce   carrot
                oats

and as many snails as you want. Think about what you would do to find out which of these foods the snails liked best.

a) Say what you would do to start with? (Draw a picture if it will help.)

b) Say how you will make sure that each food has a fair chance of being chosen:

....

....

....

c) What will you look for to decide which food was liked best?

....

....

....

4. What other things could you find out about snails by doing investigations with them?

    Write down as many things as you can think of to investigate.

    ....

    ....

    ....

    ....

5. Dan and Tammy went to visit their Aunt and looked for minibeasts in her garden. They found them all except for snails although they looked carefully for a long time.

    a) Write down any reasons you can think of to explain why there were no snails in their Aunt's garden.

        ....

        ....

        ....

    b) Their Aunt thought it could be because of the kind of soil where she lived; there was no chalk or limestone in it.

        What is the main difference between snails and other minibeasts which Dan and Tammy found?

        ....

        ....

        ....

    c) Why do you think snails only live where there is chalk or limestone in the soil?

        ....

        ....

        ....

Name .... Date of birth ....

The Sun-Dial

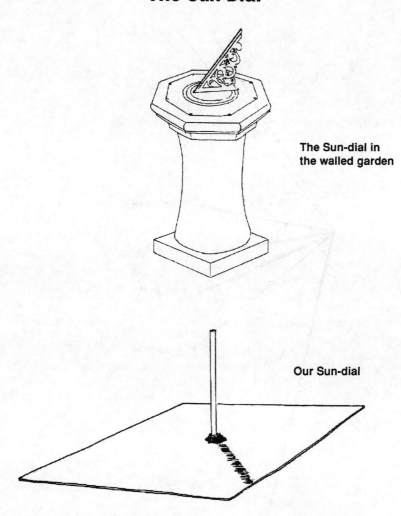

The Sun-dial in the walled garden

Our Sun-dial

You can read about sun-dials in the project folder.

The shadows on this page were marked by children during one day in August. They used the sun-dial they had made.

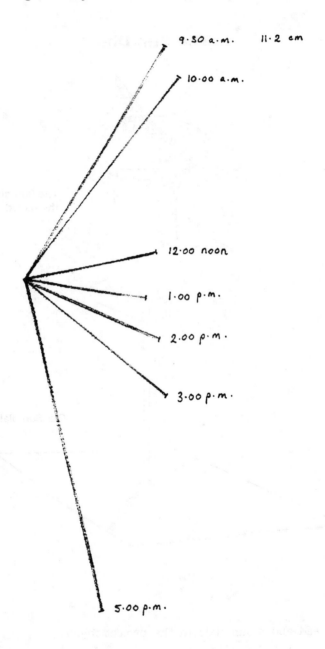

1.   Measure the shadow length at each time shown. Write the time and length in the table below.

The first one has been done for you.

Time of day   Length of shadow in cm

9.30 a.m.	11.2

2.   At 4.00 p.m. it was cloudy, so there was no shadow.

Draw in the shadow for 4.00 p.m. as you think it might have looked.

3.   How did you decide where and how to draw the shadow?

....

....

....

....

....

4.   The children also drew a graph to show their results.

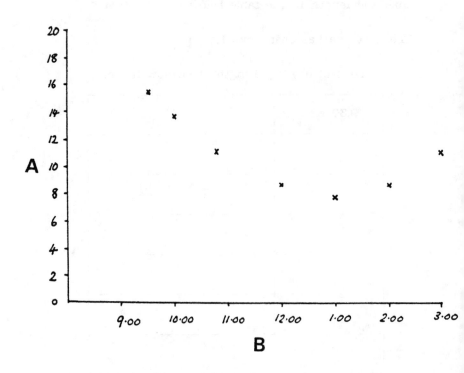

What should be written at A?

....

....

What should be written at B?

....

....

What is a good heading for this graph?

....

....

Name .... Date of birth ....

Walls

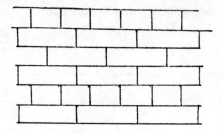

Brick patterns in the garden walls

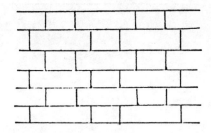

Richard and Mena were looking at walls.

1.   They noticed that some of the bricks were crumbling and
      pieces were flaking off. On one wall, there were more
      flaking, crumbling bricks at the bottom of the wall than at
      the top. Richard and Mena wondered why this might be.
      They thought of two or three possible reasons, but they
      didn't know if they were right.

      What possible reasons can you think of for the bricks being
      more crumbly at the bottom of the wall?

      Give two different reasons, and a third if you can.

      1.   ....

            ....

            ....

      2.   ....

            ....

            ....

      3.   ....

            ....

            ....

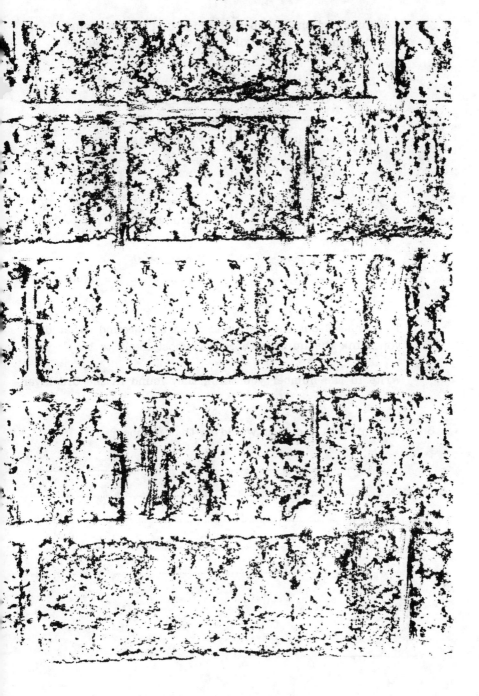

2.   They counted the number of crumbling bricks along a certain length of the wall. This is what they found:

5th layer	3 crumbling
4th layer	4 crumbling
3rd layer	
2nd layer	9 crumbling
1st layer	13 crumbling

– Ground level

They missed out the 3rd layer from the ground. What do you think the number there was most likely to be?

Write in the number you think they found in the 3rd layer.

3.   How did you decide it would be that number?

....

....

....

....

....

4. Use this piece of graph paper to draw a block graph of the number of crumbling bricks in each layer.

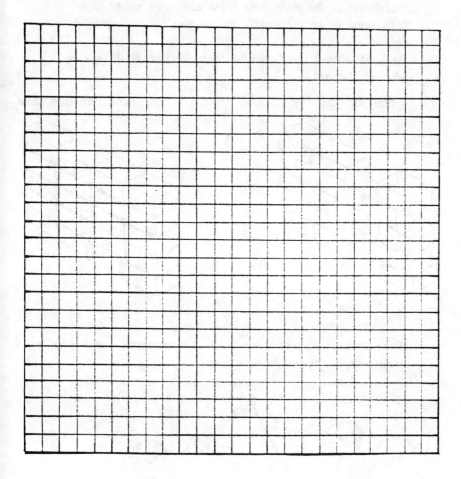

5.   When Pete and Femi looked at the other walls, they found
     that the bricks were arranged in different ways. They
     wondered if the way they were arranged made any
     difference to the strength of the walls.

     Back at school they decided to build two walls out of
     wooden bricks -

     one like this   and one like this

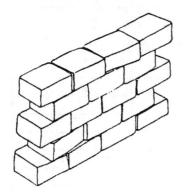
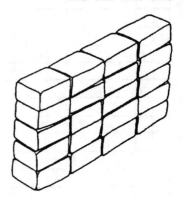

     They decided to test their walls by swinging a mass on a
     string to hit them, in this way:

a) If you were doing this, describe what you would do to test the walls with this equipment.

....

....

....

....

b) How would you decide which wall was the stronger?

....

....

....

c) How would you make sure that your test was fair?

....

....

....

6.   Pete and Femi decided to use the blocks to investigate other questions about walls (like whether a double row of bricks was twice as strong as a single row).

What other things about walls could be investigated? Write down as many as you can think of:

....

....

....

....

....

....

Name .... Date of birth ....

Water

Some of the children got splashed by the water from the
fountain as they walked by the side of the pond.

The drops soaked into their clothes quickly - not like the ducks.
When their feathers got wet they could just shake the water off.

This gave them ideas for testing fabrics to see which would be
best for keeping you dry. They tried two of these ideas later in
school.

1.   Fipst Idea

Take pieces of different fabrics and drop water onto them,
like this:

a) If you were doing the test like this, describe how you
would do it:

....

....

....

b) What would you look for to decide which was best,
which next best, and so on?

....

....

....

c) How would you make sure it was a fair test?

....

....

....

2. <u>Second Idea</u>

Put pieces of fabric over a jam jar, held by a rubber band, like this:

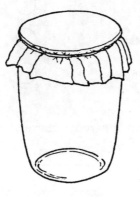

and drop water on.

a) If you were doing the test like this, describe how you would do it:

....

....

....

b) What would you look for to decide which was best, which next best, and so on?

....

....

....

c) How would you make sure it was a fair test?

....

....

....

3.   Which of these two ideas is the better way of testing the fabric do you think?

        First idea   ◯

        Second idea   ◯

        No difference   ◯

Explain the reason for your answer:

....

....

....

....

....

Name .... Date of birth ....

Wood

Over the open arch into the garden was a wooden trellis supporting climbing plants. The trellis was curved and Joan said she was surprised that wood could be bent like that without breaking. Paul thought it was a special kind of wood.

Later, at school, they were able to get some pieces of different kinds of wood to find out if some kinds bent more easily than others.

1.   They decided to take each piece and test it like this:

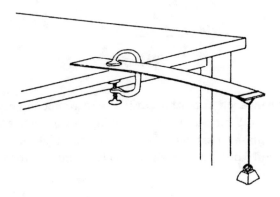

Which of these things should be different about the pieces they choose to use in their test? (Tick any you think should be different.)

The thickness of the wood ◯

The type of wood ◯

The width of the strip ◯

Where the load is hung ◯

2.   For a fair test, which of these things should they keep the same? (Tick any you think should be the same.)

The thickness of the wood   ◯

The type of wood   ◯

The width of the strip   ◯

The length of the strip   ◯

Where the load is hung   ◯

3.   What do you think they should measure or compare to decide the result?

....

....

....

....

4.   After they had tested the bendiness of the different woods,
     Joan and Paul thought of lots of other things they could
     investigate using the pieces of wood (for example, they
     thought of finding out if some kinds of wood were more
     waterproof than others).

     What other things can you think of that could be
     investigated about the pieces of wood? Write down as many
     as you can think of.

     ....

     ....

     ....

     ....

     ....

Appendix II: Walled Garden Mark Scheme

When marking Walled Garden scripts it is helpful to follow the guidelines set out below:

- Use a pencil.
- Scoring is either 1 or 0 for every question.
- Please enter the scores in the margin, adjacent to the question.
- The zeros are just as important as the ones.
- Indicate on the front cover next to the title any questions for which the response is ambiguous, in the terms of the criteria in the mark scheme.
- Where marks are allocated as *alternatives* there should be no pupils with a mark for both criteria.

Bark Rubbings

1. silver birch   Interp.   1

2. If either holly or silver birch, score 0
   sweet chestnut
   oak
   hornbeam   three of these, score 1   Interp.   1
   ash

3. holly only   Interp.   1

4. If either holly or silver birch, score 0
   sweet chestnut
   oak
   hornbeam   minimum of three of
   these scores 1   Interp.   1
   ash

5. <u>Vertical</u> pattern

   ('top to bottom', 'up and down' pattern)   Interp.   1

   Wide, deep <u>hollows</u>
   ('gaps about 2 cm', 'deep valleys')   Interp.   1

   Narrow <u>high lines</u>
   ('thin lines standing up')   Interp.   1

6. <u>Independent variable</u> (passage of time)
   A time interval, or <u>duration</u> of the experiment is   Plan Ind. Var.   1
   specified

   The overall duration is split into equal <u>intervals</u>   Plan Ind. Var.   1
   (not less than monthly)

   <u>Dependent variable</u>
   Changes to be noted in bark specified:
   e.g.   overall pattern/colour/bark rubbing
              depth of splits   Plan Dep. Var.   1
              distance between ridges

OR   **OR**

   <u>Qualitative changes</u>
   Only one to be noted: e.g. 'see if it looks different'   Plan Dep. Var.   1

   <u>Controls</u> (score maximum 3)
   Same tree   ⎫   1
   Same area of bark on that same tree   ⎬   Plan Contr.   1
   Other acceptable control(s)   ⎭   1

   <u>Quantification of dependent variables</u>
   A method of quantifying any change is specified: Plan Quant.   1
   e.g. measure length or depth of splits

Leaves

1. <u>Similarities</u> (score maximum 3)
   e.g.   both   ⎫
              green   ⎪   Obs.   1
              have stem   ⎬   Obs.   1
              have veins   ⎪   Obs.   1
              light upper, dark lower surface   ⎭

n.b. score <u>observations</u>, not recall.
'Both evergreen' is recall, score 0

<u>Differences</u> (score maximum 3)

<u>Ivy</u>		<u>Holly</u>		
glossy	-	matt	Obs.	1
blunt	-	sharp	Obs.	1
limp	-	stiff	Obs.	1

2. Judgement that all squares > 0.5 cm^2 marked, and no others — Meas. — 1

Correct total given ± 1 cm^2 — Meas. — 1

Units given (square centimetres, cm^2) — Meas. — 1

3. (a) Pattern: small at tip, larger in middle, then smaller again — Interp. Describe — 1

(b) 7 or 8 cm — Interp. Interpolate — 1

4. 19 — Record. Reading — 1

Read from *graph* — Record. Reading — 1

Extrapolation from *table* — Record. Reading — 1

5. The longer the leaf the more prickles — Interp. Describe — 1

Minibeasts

1. (a) (live) greenfly — Record. Read table — 1

(b)   They all shed their skin   Interp.   1
      'sheds skin'   Describe
      OR
      Minibeasts with legs do not lay
      their eggs in the soil

2. (a)   'Larva' in correct cell   Record.   1
                                                        Table

    (b)   'animals and plants' (both and   Record.   1
          no other) in correct cell   Table

3. The following criteria may be credited
    irrespective of where they occur
    in (a), (b) or (c).

    Independent variable (foods)   Plan
    All foods will be made available   Ind. Var   1

    Dependent variable
    Food preference operationalized:
    e.g. 'Chosen by most snails' (sequential or
          simultaneous multi-snail set-up only)
          Greatest amount/mass/volume eaten
          Most time spent eating   Plan Dep. Var.   1
          First to attract attention
OR   **OR**

    Qualitative judgement
    Food preference not specifically operationalized,   Plan   1
    e.g. 'See which food it/they like best.'   Dep. Var.

    Controls (score maximum 3)
    Foods are presented to snail(s) ....:
    e.g. equidistant from or equally accessible ⎫   1
          available in equal volume   ⎬   Plan   1
          available in equal fragments   ⎬   Contr.   1
          snails equal size   ⎭
          other reasonable control(s)

    Quantification of dependent variable
    Snail count: Plan Quant.   1
    e.g. 'See how many snails choose ....:

Measure how long spent eating, each food

Measure how much eaten, mass or volume, each food

Other quantification of dependent variable

4.	One mark for each investigable question	R.Q.		1
	(avoiding surgery!) up to maximum of three			1
	Accept general investigations and investigations of specific snails			1

No score for
Observational properties
Information giving properties
Not classifiable

5.	(a)	One mark for each reasonable hypothesis:		
		e.g. No snail food		1
		Incorrect environmental conditions	Hyp.	1
		Insecticide or other poisons		1
		up to maximum of three		
	(b)	Snails have shells	Obs.	1
	(c)	Snails need limestone to live/function (biological dependence)	Interp. Extrapolate	1
		Snails need limestone to make shells (additional mark)	Interp. Extrapolate	1

Sun-dial

1.	At least 3 times recorded in the first column (accuracy unnecessary)	Record. Table	1
	At least 3 lengths recorded in the second column (accuracy unnecessary)	Record. Table	1
	Time recording format consistent with first entry (at least 3 entries)	Record. Table	1
	Length recording format consistent with first entry (at least 3 entries)	Record. Table	1

Measurement

10.6		Meas.	1
5.7		Meas.	1
5.2	Tolerance ± 2mm	Meas.	1
6.2		Meas.	1
7.6		Meas.	1
13.9		Meas.	1

2. Angle drawn approximately bisecting those for 3.00 pm and 5.00 pm — Interp. / Interpolate — 1

Length of line within ± 5mm of a line drawn to join ends of 3.00 pm and 5.00 pm shadows — Interp. / Interpolate — 1

3. Position relates to angle between 3.00 pm and 5.00 pm shadows — Interp. / Interpolate — 1

Length between that of 3.00 pm and 5.00 pm shadows — Interp. / Interpolate — 1

4. A. Length in centimetres — Interp. — 1
    B. Time (of day) in hours — Interp. — 1
    C. Shadow length through the hours of the day/time of day — Interp. — 1 / 1

Walls

1. More exposed to physical damage by people/machines — Hyp. — 1
    plant damage
    under greater load
    water, erosion — Hyp. — 1
    exposure to sun/heat/wind
    frost damage
    Any other plausible reason up to maximum of 3 — Hyp. — 1

2. Within range 5–8 — Interp. / Interpolate — 1

Exactly 6 (additional mark)	Interp. Interpolate	1

3. 'Between 4 and 9' Interp. 1

The number crumbling increases/decreases by one more in each row (allow for expressional difficulties) (additional mark) **OR** Reference to 'pattern' and answer '6' above	Interp. Describe	1

4. One axis

Labelled 'layers' (rows, lines, etc.)	Record. Label	1
Labelled 1st, 2nd, 3rd, etc., 1, 2, 3 (at least 3 labels)	Record. Label	1
Bars equal width	Record. Construct	1
Bars equally spaced (no space, no mark)	Record. Construct	1

Other axis

Labelled 'crumbling' bricks	Record. Label	1
Labelled 'number of' (how many, etc)	Record. Label	1
Equal interval scale (one division has equal value throughout)	Record. Construct	1
Scale labelled with numbers (spaces or divisions)	Record. Construct	1

Plotting
(Credit co-ordination of axes as drawn)

1st layer	13	Record. Plot	1
2nd layer	9	Record. Plot	1

4th layer	4		Record. Plot	1
5th layer	3		Record. Plot	1

The following criteria may be credited irrespective of where they occur in (a), (b) or (c)

5. <u>Independent variable</u> (wall structure)   Plan   1
   Use 2 walls having different pattern   Ind. Var.

   <u>Dependent variable</u> (strength of wall)   Plan   1
   Criterion for 'stronger' specified   Dep. Var.

OR   **OR**

   <u>Qualitative judgement</u>   Plan   1
   'See which is stronger'   Dep. Var.

   <u>Controls</u> (score maximum 3)
   Same number of bricks in each wall   1

   Same mass   Plan   1
                      Contr.

   Path of mass controlled   1

   Other reasonable control

   <u>Quantification of dependent variable</u>
   Damage measured, e.g. <u>number</u> of bricks   Plan   1
   displaced, <u>distance</u> or <u>angle</u> of displacement   Quant.
   OR
   <u>number</u> of hits to demolish

6. One mark for each <u>investigable</u> question or   R.Q.   1
   problem raised, to maximum of 3.   1
                                                                  1

   Credit investigation of <u>real</u> walls or <u>block</u> walls.

   <u>No score for</u>
   Observational features
   Information giving statements
   Unclassifiable statements

Water

The same mark scheme is used for questions 1 and 2. The following criteria may be credited irrespective of where they occur in (a), (b) or (c).

1. Independent variable (type of fabric)
    State use of at least two different fabrics   Plan   1
             Ind. Var.

    Dependent variable (waterproof-ness defined or operationalized)

    Decide degree to which fabrics . . . . :
    e.g. absorb water   Plan   1
          let water pass through   Dep. Var.
          are impermeable

OR   OR

    Qualitative judgement
    'Look for the least wet'   Plan   1
           Dep. Var.

    Controls (score up to maximum of 3)
    e.g. amount of water   Plan   1
          application of water (height, method, etc.)   Contr.   1
          other reasonable control(s)   1

    Quantification of dependent variable
    e.g. Measure mass (absorbed, retained,   Plan   1
             going through)   Quant.
          Measure volume (retained or
             going through)
          Measure area of water stain
          Measure time to reach criterion effect, etc.

2. Use criteria as for Question 1, above

3. Critical Reflection on the two procedures:
    A comment to the effect that each of the two   C.R.   1
    procedures was an acceptable fair test

OR   OR

    A preference for one investigation over the other   C.R.   1
    expressed in operational or measurement terms
    (not just personal preference)

Wood

1. The type of wood   Plan   1
                                                          Ind. Var.

2. The type of wood   Plan   1
                                                          Contr.

3. How much the wood bends   Plan   1
                                                          Dep. Var.

4. One mark for each investigable question,   1
    concerning the properties of wood to maximum   R.Q.   1
    of three   1

    No score for
    Observational features
    Information giving statements
    Other unclassifiable responses
        (e.g. incomprehensible, irrelevant)

References

Cavendish, S., Galton, M., Hargreaves, L. and Harlen, W. (1990) *Assessing Science in the Primary Classroom: Observing Activities*, Paul Chapman Publishing, London.

Davis, B. (1983) The problems of starting and continuing primary science, advanced diploma thesis, Department of Educational Studies, University of Oxford.

DES (1978) *Primary Education in England*, HMSO, London.

DES (1980) *Mathematical Development. APU Primary Survey Report No. 1*, HMSO, London.

DES (1984) *APU Science Report for Teachers: 4. Science Assessment Framework, Age 11*, Harlen, W. Palacio, D. and Russell, T. ASE, Hatfield.

DES (1985) *Science 5–16: A Statement of Policy*, HMSO, London.

DES (1986) *APU Science Report for Teachers: 8. Planning Scientific Investigations at Age 11*, Harlen, W. ASE, Hatfield.

DES (1987) *National Curriculum Science Working Group. Interim Report*, DES and WO, London.

DES (1988) *A Report. National Curriculum Task Group on Assessment and Testing*, DES and WO, London.

DES (1989) *Science at Age 11. A Review of APU Survey Findings 1980–1984*, Russell, T. (ed.) HMSO, London.

Donaldson, M. (1978) *Children's Minds*, Collins, Glasgow.

Ennever, L. and Harlen, W. (1972) *With Objectives in Mind: Guide to Science 5–13*, Macdonald Educational, London.

Galton, M. and Patrick, H. (1990) *Curriculum Provision in the Small Primary School*, Routledge, London.

Galton, M., Simon, B. and Croll, P. (1980) *Inside the Primary Classroom*, Routledge & Kegan Paul, London.

Harlen, W. (1983) *Guides to Assessment in Education: Science*, Macmillan, London.

Harlen, W. (1985a) Planning, running and following through a workshop in

England, in Harlen, W. (ed.) *The Training of Primary Science Educators – A Workshop Approach*, UNESCO, Paris.

Harlen, W. (1985b) *Teaching and Learning Primary Science*, Paul Chapman Publishing, London.

Harlen, W., Darwin, A. and Murphy, M. (1977) *Match and Mismatch: Raising Questions*: Oliver & Boyd, Edinburgh.

Hawking, S. W. (1988) *A Brief History of Time*, Bantam Press, London.

Hughes, M. (1986) *Children and Number*, Blackwell, Oxford.

McGough, R. (1985) *Who, Why, Where, What*, Deutsch, London.

Parker, S. (1983) The preparation of teachers for primary school science, in Harlen, W. (ed.) *New Trends in Primary School Science Education*, UNESCO, Paris.

Russell, T. and Harlen, W. (1990) *Assessing Science in the Primary Classroom: Practical Tasks*, Paul Chapman Publishing, London.

Stenhouse, L. (1975) *An Introduction to Curriculum Research and Development*, Heinemann, London.

Wood, D. (1988) *How Children Think and Learn*, Blackwell, Oxford.

Index